WHAT DO YOU DO WHEN...

- He complains he can't make friends
- She won't eat anything but peanut butter
- A tantrum erupts every time you say "no"
- Bedtime is a nightly struggle
- She refuses to wear her jacket—even when it's snowing
- He "hates" everything
- Others are criticizing your child—and criticizing you too
- You feel you can't do anything right

If this sounds like your child, then read on. *The Demanding Child* will not only help you understand why your child can be so difficult, it will offer you sound, caring advice on helping him—and you—cope with life's daily challenges.

Also by Janet Poland
The Magical Years series

GETTING TO KNOW YOUR ONE-YEAR-OLD
SURVIVING YOUR TWO-YEAR-OLD
MAKING FRIENDS WITH YOUR THREE-YEAR-OLD

The Challenging Child series

THE SENSITIVE CHILD

THE CHALLENGING CHILD SERIES

THE
DEMANDING
CHILD

JANET POLAND

JUDI CRAIG, PH.D.,
Consulting Editor

A Skylight Press Book

St. Martin's Paperbacks

Published by arrangement with Skylight Press, 260 West 72nd Street, Suite 6-C, New York, N.Y. 10023. (212) 874-4348

THE CHALLENGING CHILD: THE DEMANDING CHILD

Copyright © 1996 by Skylight Press.

Cover photograph by Peter Brandt.

ISBN: 0-312-96054-9

Printed in the United States of America

St. Martin's Paperbacks edition/December 1996

10 9 8 7 6 5 4 3 2 1

Contents

Foreword

Do you have the kind of child for whom even the word *difficult* is an understatement? The kind of youngster who makes you wish—at times—that you could just get on a plane to a marvelous place and never come back to reality? The kid who drains you physically and emotionally so that you fall into bed at night feeling like a dishrag?

Hold on. There is help.

In *The Demanding Child*, Janet Poland shows you that you are not alone. Millions of kids fit into the "demanding" category. This means that millions of parents often feel like inadequate mothers and fathers, receive dirty looks in public for the way their children behave, and get criticism—if not out-right blame—from well-intentioned relatives and friends.

Poland first divides "demanding" children into four categories: high energy, impulsive, angry and persistent/insatiable. And, of course, the categories aren't necessarily mutually exclusive (unfortunately!). She then cites research on temperament, which gives a rich perspective on how biological makeup and environmental experiences shape the demanding child's behavior.

In the chapter on why raising a demanding child is *so* demanding, readers will readily identify with the normal reactions parents inevitably have to the challenges before them. How a fit—or a misfit—between a child's temperament and a parent's is well described, followed by a chapter that thoughtfully examines how demanding children look at their world "from the inside."

So how can a parent help? Poland lists twenty well-meaning mistakes parents of such children commonly make, then discusses more specifically the parent errors for each of the four types. The chapters that follow give sound, practical tips on handling a child's anger and dealing with specific environments and situations when demanding kids are more likely to run into difficulty.

Although the positive side of the demanding child's temperament is mentioned throughout the book, one chapter deals specifically with what the future holds for these children. This discussion will free parents from seeing their child's future based on their current parenting struggles, and allow them to feel positive and hopeful about their child's adulthood. Commonly asked questions and answers follow.

Like *The Sensitive Child*, Poland's companion book, *The Demanding Child*, is informative and clearly practical. It will also come as a welcome re-lief to parents of demanding children!

Judi Craig, Ph.D.
Clinical Psychologist, Author and Speaker

THE
DEMANDING
CHILD

Understanding the Demanding Child: Recognizing and Interpreting Your Child's Behavior

"I used to be a good mother. That's the way I thought of myself. Melissa was so easy at this stage. All along, I thought it was because I was doing a wonderful job raising her.

"And then Nick was born . . ."

From birth, Nick was a whirring turbine of energy. He squirmed and fussed all day and most of the night. His parents were convinced he never slept. Just diapering him was a wrestling match. He pulled himself up at eight months of age, walked (and immediately ran) at ten months, and hasn't stopped since.

Now he's five, and still going strong. He's bright and ready for kindergarten, but is kindergarten ready for him? His parents wonder: Will he be able to sit at a desk? Will he make and keep friends? Will he hurt himself or get in trouble at school?

Nick's parents worry about Nick and about his future. But they aren't just worried. They're *tired*—physically tired and emotionally stressed.

That's because Nick is a demanding child. The first book in this series, *The Sensitive Child*, discussed the nature and needs of children who are more shy, anxious, or cautious than their peers. This book deals with the sensitive child's alter ego: the bouncy, energetic, defiant, whiney, aggressive, impulsive, stubborn, intrusive, exhausting boy or girl we call the demanding child.

Demanding children are difficult to raise because they demand more of parents. They demand more of teachers, friends, neighbors—more of life itself. They call into question a parent's self-confidence, judgment, even sanity.

But demanding children are normal. They're healthy kids whose temperament puts them on one end of the behavioral spectrum. They're often spunky, spirited, creative, and funny. They can and do thrive, and they can have bright futures. But that future is more precarious than it is with easier children. To a great extent, it depends on whether parents hinder their child's development or guide it in positive directions. The key is to know what makes the demanding child tick, and know what approaches are effective and which are not. That's what this book is about.

There's nothing unusual, of course, about a child with lots of energy, a toddler who explodes with anger, or a preschooler who whines. These behaviors come with the territory of childhood. But the demanding child is *more so*. More intense. More energetic. More stubborn. More demanding of time and attention.

The demanding child oversteers. When others

talk, he bellows. When others dawdle, he is an immovable object. When others pout, he rages.

"I have one child, but I feel as if I have triplets," said one mother. "Justin is three times as active as other children; he makes three times as much noise and mess. He's always demanding, complaining, arguing. I worry about him all the time. Sometimes I feel overwhelmed. How can I keep up with his intensity?"

THE CHALLENGE OF RAISING A DEMANDING CHILD

Parents of demanding children struggle with three essential challenges:

• First, they frequently are unaware of what aspects of their child's behavior can be changed and what most likely cannot. So they engage in a doomed struggle to "improve" or "cure" their child on one hand, or throw up their hands in defeat on the other.

• Second, parents worry about the future of their family and of their challenging child. How will they get through the next year—or the next week? Will their impulsive, high-energy son become a juvenile delinquent? Will their stubborn daughter drive away her friends? The anxieties parents have, and the negative ways they often describe their children, can taint the parenting process and diminish the child's self-image.

• Finally, they must live with and try to cope with a child who is resistant to the kind of useful advice that works fairly well with most children.

Like Nick's parents, they often find that the parental skills that proved successful with Child Number One are ineffectual when Child Number Two is demanding.

The purpose of this book is to help parents take on those challenges. As the parent of a demanding child, you'll find your effectiveness will increase when you:

• Recognize the demanding personality and the different ways it expresses itself. Once you have identified your child's particular style, you'll be better able to support his development and guide his behavior.

• Sort out what parts of your child's behavior are likely to endure, and which aspects can be altered or modified. By doing so you'll avoid the futile effort of trying to teach your child to be something he's not. If your child is highly energetic, he's likely to stay that way; you're better off trying to direct his energy rather than seeking to turn him into a serene, quiet child.

• Recognize that other parents experience the same frustrations and react in similar ways—and that some of those natural reactions may actually hinder your child's development. Raising a demanding child takes a toll, and you'll be better able to maintain your patience and perspective when you realize that you are not alone.

• Redefine your child's personality to accentuate the positive. Demanding behavior has its advantages and disadvantages. When you celebrate your child's unique strengths, two good things happen: You begin to look at your child in a more positive light, and he begins to view himself with more pride and confidence.

• Help your child cope with the challenges and difficulties of his personality. You'll learn ways to direct his energy, buffer his impulsiveness, and defuse his anger.

• Learn to handle the personality clashes that occur when you and your child have strikingly different temperaments. It's tough to cope with an energetic, outgoing, intrusive child who never gives up, when you, his parent, are quiet, contemplative, cautious, and anxious.

• Learn to recognize, and work with, specific settings and situations that are difficult for your child. Often, demanding children are at their most challenging in the classroom or playground but not at home. Others play well in small groups but lose control in large groups or on an athletic team.

• Find ways of meeting your own needs, and those of your spouse and other family members. Demanding children can be exhausting, and you as a parent need to maintain your strength and your spirits.

• Help your child understand and modify his own behavior. The more he understands his own personality, the more he can predict situations that will cause him trouble. The more you've helped him broaden his skills and gain some control of his temper or of his impulses, the more able he will be to take over the task of helping *himself* behave more appropriately.

In this book, we will discuss children who are

still coming to terms with their temperament birthright.

Generally, we're focusing on children who have left infancy behind but have not yet reached adolescence. By about age three, it's becoming possible to diagnose innate personality traits. Before that, it's a bit difficult; after all, what infant or toddler *isn't* demanding?

And adolescents bring their own issues of separation and challenge into play. In Chapter 9, we'll discuss the future of your demanding child as an adolescent and as an adult, but this book focuses on the years in between toddlerhood and adolescence, when children are gradually developing their muscles, their intellectual skills, and their emotional strength and independence. You, as the parent of a demanding child, will be the primary force (along with teachers and other influential adults) in guiding this development, day by day.

Naturally, both boys and girls can be demanding. High energy is more common among boys; insatiability among girls. In this book, we refer to children generally as "he" in odd-numbered chapters, "she" in the even ones. But the suggestions of course apply to all demanding children.

WHAT'S BEHIND DEMANDING BEHAVIOR

This series is about those children whose distinct temperament brings particular difficulties; both the sensitive child, discussed in the companion volume, and the demanding child, require a different approach toward discipline, social experiences, emotional support, and the building of self-esteem and confidence.

That's because—according to the most recent findings in psychology, neurology, and genetics—temperament is as much a part of a child's innate individuality as the color of his hair or the shape of his nose.

And these rich differences in human temperament reflect traits that have endured through the generations because they have survival value. The wary, cautious early human sensed danger and was adept at avoiding risk; his fearless cousin ventured into the unknown, explored new territory, and defended it against enemies.

Temperament affects how we approach other people, how we respond to limits, how we handle our fears and our anger. For that reason, we need to take it into account when we discipline our children, comfort them, and introduce them to the world. And we need to talk to our children about temperament and teach them ways to make the most of their gifts.

Whether you have one child or five, your understanding of the role of temperament will help you in your efforts to be a wise, understanding and effective parent.

Demanding children differ, as we'll discuss later in this chapter. But they have similarities as well:

1. Their behavior seems more so: *more* energetic, *more* stubborn, *more* aggressive, *more* noisy, or *more* intense. If the sensitive children we dis-

cussed in the first book of The Challenging Child series tended to retreat and hold back, the demanding child makes himself seen and heard in no uncertain terms.

2. Demanding children are, usually, demanding from infancy and will probably remain so, to some degree, throughout life. A tranquil, easily soothed infant who becomes demanding and defiant at age two is probably exhibiting typical toddler behavior, not the enduring temperament traits we discuss here.

3. Demanding behavior can bring both problems and blessings, depending on how parents structure their children's lives and help them manage and perceive their own behavior.

WHY THE CONVENTIONAL WISDOM DOESN'T WORK

Too often, advice about raising children assumes they all come from the same mold. Tantrums, toilet training, and nightmares all get one-size-fits-all recommendations. But, as any parent of more than one child can attest—and Nick's parents would second—that's rarely realistic. One approach to tantrums, nightmares, or toilet training may work with the older child and fail completely with the second.

If your cautious, eager-to-please older child forgets the rules, you can probably do very well with a gentle reminder: "John, remember that baseballs belong outside, not in the living room."

If John's little brother is a fearless, impulsive, combative bundle of energy, however, your gentle reminder may be woefully inadequate with him.

If your older, less demanding child wants your undivided attention, you can meet his needs with some conversation and perhaps a board game or a half-hour of stories. But if you try to satisfy your demanding child's need for attention, he consumes your every waking moment.

If you try to apply the same approach to temper tantrums that succeeded with your your older children, it collapses in the face of the hissing spitfire your demanding child becomes when he's furious.

Many of us, as parents, rely on the standard wisdom that we should praise and encourage our children when they behave well, and try to downplay or ignore undesirable behavior. And it's the right approach for most children: Children tend to repeat the behavior that we reward with our attention and affection.

But the demanding child often persists in behavior that seems to offer no reward, long after another child might have abandoned it. He'll whine and nag relentlessly. He'll defy you even though experience tells him it's useless. He'll smash another child's sand castle even though he knows he'll be ostracized from the group. He'll jump from a garden wall even though last week he hurt his ankle doing the same thing. This trait is especially evident in the persistent child (whom we discuss below), but it shows itself in various guises among most demanding children.

For this reason, relying on "natural consequences" to guide behavior is likely to fall short when your child is demanding. Your task will be to structure consequences so they are most effective in guiding his particular style of challenging behavior.

In addition, demanding children may have a higher pain or discomfort threshold than other children. Sensitive children, as discussed in the first book of this series, probably have a neurological basis for their greater physical and emotional sensitivity; demanding and "difficult" children may also have a biological basis to their hard-charging personalities and their resistance to distraction or deflection. We'll examine these foundations in more detail in Chapter 2.

Challenging children require wise guidance, direction, and limits. They need to develop self-esteem and skills. They need help understanding themselves, and learning how to direct their own style in ways that will ultimately prove fulfilling to them.

IDENTIFYING YOUR DEMANDING CHILD'S STYLE

Much of the current body of knowledge about temperament and children is attributable to the work of Stella Chess and Alexander Thomas, two psychologists who initiated one of the first studies of temperament, the New York Longitudinal Study, in 1956. They began with a group of infants and followed their development at regular intervals until most were adolescents (they are continuing to study the group into adulthood). What they concluded was that different temperaments are observable early in life, persist throughout childhood, and call for specific child-rearing techniques.

Chess and Thomas categorized their group of children into "easy," "slow-to-warm-up," and "difficult," depending on the distribution of nine temperamental traits:

- Activity level (general level of physical energy and movement, usually evident from infancy)
- Rhythmicity (regularity of functions like eating, sleeping, elimination)
- Approach or withdrawal (the initial response to new situations)
- Adaptability (the ease with which the child adjusts to transitions and changes in routine)
- Sensory threshold (how sensitive the child is to light, noise, strong flavors, rough textures)
- Quality of mood (generally pleasant, or generally negative)
- Intensity of reaction (the strength of emotional responses, both happy and unhappy)
- Distractability (the ability to focus and pay attention)
- Persistence (the tendency to stay with one activity, whether positive or negative, for a long time)

Certainly an "easy" child would be cheerful, not overly active, reasonably regular in habits, and not too fussy about food and clothing.

"Slow-to-warm-up" describes a child with negative initial reaction and slow adaptability. Many sensitive children have those qualities, along with a low sensory threshold and a high persistence.

"Difficult" children might include children who are unusually energetic, irregular in habits and rhythms, and who have great difficulty adapting to change. The demanding children who are the subject of this book are indeed the "difficult" children in this category. Our categories also include the kind of persistence that borders on insatiability: the negative, whining, stubborn child who doesn't know when to stop.

For the purpose of this book, we're breaking demanding behavior down into four categories that reflect recent scientific insights into temperament. Each of the following demanding categories represents a predisposition that is probably rooted in biology, and thus each style calls calls for a different parenting approach.

A high-energy, demanding child who is fairly cheerful and cooperative, on the whole, needs different techniques from the child who is aggressive and hostile, or the child who is relentless, persistent, and prone to complaining or whining.

THE HIGH-ENERGY CHILD

Jack and Laura have a large backyard that's ideal for their three children to play in. They've always encouraged plenty of unrestricted outdoor play so their children could "let off steam," and return to the house tired and relaxed. Then came Eric.

When Eric lets off steam, he doesn't seem to release any pressure. He can manage better, in fact, when he's tightly controlled—he's fine in a barber's chair or even an airplane seat, but once he starts to loosen up, he loosens so totally that he loses all control and ends up either getting hurt, breaking something, or screaming so loud he loses his voice.

Eric never runs out of steam himself because someone always intervenes to prevent mayhem or keep him from getting hurt.

The high-energy child has his throttle set to "full speed ahead" all the time. His pedal is always to the metal. Everything he does is physical and energetic. When others walk, he runs. In school, he squirms, fidgets, and drums his fingers. He never runs out of steam until he drops from exhaustion.

Often, he doesn't know his own strength. Instead of giving you a hug, he crushes you in a bearlike embrace. If he doesn't realize that the door is locked when he tries to open it, he pulls the knob right off.

Often, the the high-energy child is cheerful and cooperative; his behavior may be boisterous but not aggressive or hostile. Usually, it's the sheer boundlessness of his physical energy that makes him demanding.

Your child may fall under the high energy category if he:

- Was a fussy baby who didn't sleep much
- Was an early walker
- Is constantly "on the go"
- Seems more energetic than other children his age

- Hates to sit still or be confined
- Usually makes more noise than other children
- Is athletic or enjoys sports

HYPERACTIVITY

It's important to mention the distinction between high-energy children, as we discuss them here, and children diagnosed with ADHD, or Attention Deficit Hyperactivity Disorder.

Generally, children with ADHD are highly energetic but also have difficulty focusing that energy. They tend to have a hard time concentrating in school and managing their behavior. In the classroom, for example, a child with ADHD is likely to fidget and squirm, and fail to focus effectively on his work. A demanding child with high energy, by contrast, does manage to focus his energy. He may be just as fidgety and squirmy, but he'll get the job done.

A diagnosis of ADHD requires an evaluation from professionals in this field. Usually, they will adhere to the American Psychiatric Association's criteria for the disorder.

The criteria for the Hyperactive/Impulsive subtype of ADHD are as follows:

The child exhibits at least six of the following symptoms for at least six months, and to a degree that impairs social or academic functioning. Also, some of the behaviors have to have been present before the age of seven, and appear in two or more settings, such as school and home. The child often:

- Fidgets or squirms
- Can't stay in his seat at school
- Runs and climbs excessively and inappropriately
- Has trouble playing quietly
- Is "on the go"
- Talks excessively
- Blurts out answers before hearing questions
- Has trouble waiting his turn
- Interrupts or intrudes

The treatment of ADHD usually involves a combination of medication and behavioral techniques. However, many of the techniques for managing energetic kids and helping them gain control and a sense of self-worth apply to a range of energetic children, whether they've been diagnosed with ADHD or not.

If you think your child's uncontrollable energy and difficulty in learning and managing his behavior are severe, he should be evaluated for ADHD.

THE IMPULSIVE CHILD

Everything Matt does is quick and explosive. He no sooner thinks about crossing the room than he's there, bumping into the wall. He's in the street before his brain has a chance to tell him, "Whoa! Wait for cars!"

Emotionally, he's intense. If he's happy, he's totally happy, and if he's sad or angry, you can tell immediately. Matt slams doors. He breaks glasses by putting them down too hard. He spills because his movements are naturally abrupt.

"When Matt was little, I was always cleaning chocolate milk out of his ears," his mother recalls. "He'd grab the cup, tilt his head back and hurl it down his throat and all over his face. He couldn't just move the cup to his lips like everyone else!"

A camp counselor who is a keen observer of children can tell when she's dealing with impulsive children.

"They stand out from the other kids who are just energetic," she says. "They are the ones who always get stickers and thorns—they grab things before they can think. When we play ball, they're the ones who always run for the base even though they *know* they can't make it. They blast off before they've had a chance to count down."

Impulsivity can lead a child into trouble even when he means well. When Robert's fourth-grade class first began to go to the computer room, his fingers would take on a life of their own, poking at keyboards and flipping switches. Soon screens would blink and printers would clatter and teachers would shout, "No, Robert! Don't touch yet!"

School can be a challenge for impulsive children like Robert and Matt. When other children raise their hands, they shout out answers. They interrupt. They're always grabbing things from other children's desks, talking out loud.

Like the high-energy child, the impulsive child's behavior may not be negative. Whether he gets tangled up in nettles, plunges into the pool without checking the temperature, or bursts into tears when something makes him upset, his behavior seems instantaneous.

Your demanding child may be impulsive if he:

- Moves abruptly; darts from place to place
- Leaps before looking
- Is unusually careless
- Gets hurt frequently
- Spills and breaks things more frequently than most children
- Speaks without thinking, cries or becomes angry easily
- Interrupts more than other children
- Has trouble waiting
- Has trouble resisting temptation
- Often seems genuinely surprised by what he's done wrong

THE ANGRY CHILD

Nicole is an intense eight-year-old who responds to frustration with outbursts of rage. Just about anything can set her off: Being asked to turn off the television and start her homework. Getting up to the ticket window and finding the movie is sold out.

Nicole's parents had relied on traditional methods of discipline: explaining the rules, issuing warnings, and enforcing consequences when she misbehaved.

But Nicole's behavior doesn't respond well to rational rules and rational consequences. She gets to a point where she seems *incapable* of controlling herself, and no amount of punishment helps her gain that control.

"We can tell when she's on the way to going ballistic," said Nicole's father. "She gives us lots of warning signals. Her voice gets more shrill, and her whole body gets clenched. If we issue a stern demand when she's like that, it's hopeless. We have better luck showing some sympathy *before* things get out of hand. We'll say, 'Looks like you're feeling a lot of pressure right now and you need a place to calm down.' Or, we'll suggest she go outside and shoot baskets for a while."

Angry children like Nicole are emotionally intense. Like impulsive children, they express their emotions easily. But the angry child's outburst is different. It has an element of hostility that's usually lacking in impulsive outbursts. The impulsive child's outburst is over quickly, like a summer thunderstorm. Not so for the angry child.

If two kindergarten children get in trouble for hitting, the impulsive child really "didn't mean to"—it just *happened*. The child may have an expression of surprise and remorse about what happened.

But the angry child *isn't* sorry, at least in the heat of the moment. He may say, "He started it!" And he's likely to stay angry.

Your demanding child may be angry if he:

- Has frequent tantrums
- Is defiant
- Shows a low tolerance for frustration
- Has bouts of anger that don't blow over; he may brood or stew about negative feelings
- Hits or punches more than other children
- Sometimes has trouble maintaining friendships because of his temper
- Sometimes provokes his own anger and keeps it boiling

A short temper is part of the normal range of human temperament. It can be managed and guided into directions that are constructive, not destructive. Sometimes anger is so intense, so profound, and so debilitating that it becomes disabling. We deal with these more complex kinds of anger in Chapter 7.

THE PERSISTENT CHILD

The persistent child has trouble with limits. He's impossible to satisfy. If he starts complaining, he'll complain all day. If he wants attention, he'll never seem to get enough.

"We always tried to give our children enough of our time and attention so they felt sustained and secure," said one mother. "Elena and I would spend hours reading or playing a game in an unhurried way. Besides being enjoyable for both of us, I always felt that the time paid off in her ability to be comfortable and secure doing things away from us.

"But with Sara, *nothing* is ever enough. If we try to fill her need, there's no end to it. The more she gets, the more she wants, and it never ends. After hours of playing together, I feel entitled to a few minutes of time to myself."

Seven-year-old Lauren monopolizes her teacher's time with her requests for attention and approval. "Is this right? Don't you like mine? Do you like my dress?" She's the same way with her friends, constantly demanding proof that they like her, that she's pretty. Her teacher says, "There's never enough attention. She has to be on top of you every minute. Like she can't get enough, no matter what. The cup never fills."

This insatiability may come in many forms. It masquerades as ingratitude. "I just bought you an ice cream cone," grumbles a father, "and now you want a balloon too. What next?"

Joshua has had four friends over to celebrate his eleventh birthday with pizza, videos, and a sleepover. Late the next morning, when the kids have just left, his parents expect some peace and quiet. What does Joshua do? He heads for the phone and invites another friend over for more noise and excitement.

This style of demanding behavior is marked by the child's difficulty with limits. Sometimes the limits have to do with knowing when he's satisfied. Most of us have internal settings that cue us when we have eaten enough, or exercised enough, or played enough. When we're satisfied, we stop what we're doing and move on to a different activity. But the persistent, insatiable child just keeps on and on.

This difficulty with limits can extend to more concrete boundaries as well. This is the child who constantly bursts into occupied bathrooms, invades the privacy of parents in their bedroom, wanders into neighbors' houses.

Once the persistent child gets going, he's relentless and nearly impossible to dislodge. He nags, he whines. He gets stuck, locked in.

The persistent child brings a particular challenge to parents because it interferes with the natural reward of being a parent. When your baby fusses and cries, you feed and soothe him. Then he settles down and smiles at you. That's your reward. Or you please your five-year-old, and he gives you a warm hug. These cues that we have succeeded in satisfying our child pay us back for all the things that we do for our children. But the insatiable child seldom pays up, because to him we haven't delivered. Whatever we do is not enough.

Your demanding child may fall under the persistent category if he:

- Gets "stuck"—particularly in negative ways, like complaining or whining
- Never seems to have enough of anything—attention, toys, treats, excitement, horseplay
- Tends toward a loss of control: Horseplay leads to violence, humor and silliness lead to screeching hysterics in the restaurant, loud voices become deafening

• Is nosy and intrusive about other people's business, their possessions, or their space

Some demanding children exhibit more than one trait, and there is of course overlap. An energetic child may seem almost insatiable in his ability to keep on the go. The angry child may be negative and complaining and refuse to let his anger go.

Your demanding child, of course, may possess only one of these characteristics, or several. But whatever kind of demanding behavior your child exhibits, one thing is likely to emerge from this description: Some traits appear positive, some traits appear to present challenges. That is one of the keys to understanding this behavior, and temperament in general. Nearly every temperamental trait can be a strength, if it's recognized, identified in positive terms, moderated when necessary, and accepted by the child as part of his unique human endowment.

If your child's individuality is a loom, with half the threads present from birth, it is a loom on which you, as parents, weave experiences and attitudes and memories into those fundamental biological strands. This book is about the warp and weft of your challenging child's personality, and your role in creating that tapestry.

◆ 2 ◆

The Origins of Challenging Behavior: How Biology and Experience Shape Temperament

Just as wise parents have always known that children arrive in the world endowed with their own unique personalities, philosophers and scientists over the centuries have observed these differences and struggled to explain them.

Humans have been studying temperament as long as there have been human beings. People have scrutinized the personality quirks of their neighbors as long as there have been neighbors to scrutinize. Why is one neighbor consistently angry and vengeful, while another is easygoing, sociable, and cheerful? Why do two sisters respond so differently to poverty or misfortune: one is crushed, yet the other manages to cope and thrive despite adversity?

These are old questions, and for thousands of years we have hungered for explanations. Because of that hunger, we have occasionally swallowed explanations that have not withstood the test of time. Today, however, we have more means than ever for finding and evaluating answers—and greater opportunities for understanding what makes our children the way they are.

A SHORT HISTORY OF TEMPERAMENT

The history of our understanding of human personality and temperament is not one of unalloyed progress. Some views that once held sway seem silly to us today, and those we hold today may well be modified in time. Through the centuries, the pendulum has swung back and forth between an emphasis on biology to an emphasis on environment. And with each swing of the pendulum, sound concepts may be cast out along with invalid ones, only to be rediscovered later.

The classical view

In Western civilization, attitudes toward temperament were shaped for millennia by the classical views of the Greeks. The ancient physicians Hippocrates and Galen classified the array of human personalities in terms of "humours"—fluids within the body that, when properly balanced, yielded the ideal well-adjusted personality. Imbalances, in the form of an excess of one of these four humours, produced specific temperamental extremes.

In this view, the sanguine person, governed by the influence of blood, was cheerful and outgoing (much like the extroverted, energetic "people person" of today).

The choleric type, influenced by an excess of choler, or "yellow bile," was aggressive and easily angered.

The phlegmatic person (influenced by phlegm, or, in later centuries, lymph), was stoic, calm, and self-possessed.

And, finally, the melancholic temperament was created by an excess of black bile, yielding a shy, sad, introverted sort.

The idea that body fluids control personality may seem quaint today, but the influence of these categories endured in the Western world well into the eighteenth century. Even today, we allude to them when we refer to someone whose outlook is sanguine or melancholic or bilious or phlegmatic. And we still talk of the hot blood of the passionate and the cold blood of the merciless.

With the flourishing of science and philosophy during the Enlightenment, however, these views finally became subject to closer scrutiny. Eighteenth-century advances in medicine and anatomy opened up an interest in the structure of the brain and nervous system. New philosophical and political views championed ideas of human freedom and social and political opportunity. The classical approach to human nature began to seem rigid and limiting.

The uses and misuses of science

By the 1800s, science dominated the study of temperament. New theories and explanations of human nature arose from discoveries in anatomy, archeology, genetics, and evolution. Investigators eagerly looked beyond blood and bile to study the relative size of brain structures, the structure of the skeleton, the shape of the head, the pigmentation of the skin.

The hidden mysteries of temperament, personality, and even virtue, it was believed, had to leave some physical evidence on the human body. And so scientists went to work with scales, calipers, charts and graphs, hoping to detect disease, measure intelligence, determine personality, predict criminal behavior, and assess character.

By the early twentieth century, the Eugenics movement championed these approaches as a way of improving humankind. By defining and measuring the "ideal" type, one could then define and measure "inferior" types, and limit their influence by restricting their immigration or discouraging reproduction.

Not surprisingly, the "ideal" human being always seemed to bear a remarkable resemblance to the people doing the defining. And—again, not surprisingly—the excesses of the Eugenics movement were enthusiastically embraced by political leaders with agendas of their own.

By the 1930s, fascist leaders were proclaiming the

superiority of the Aryan "ideal" specimen and the scientifically provable "inferiority" of other types. After World War II, the world was so repelled by the implications of biological evaluations of human traits that the scientific community turned away from most research into temperament.

Psychological views of temperament

At the same time, psychiatrists, psychologists, and other researchers were looking at other sources of explanation for human behavior in all its variety. During the same decades that the Eugenics movement was concentrating on biological differences, psychology was looking closely at the influence of the environment on personality.

Behaviorists, influenced by the pioneering work of Ivan Pavlov, argued that behavior was learned, not innate. It was, they said, molded by early childhood experience, not by inborn balances of fluids, inherited body shape, or head bumps.

In their view, children behave in certain ways not because of innate physical differences but in response to rewards and punishments, positive and negative experiences. Thus the aggressive, unmanageable child is that way because her parents have failed to provide the proper positive or negative reinforcements, like limits, on one hand, and support and praise, on the other.

The behaviorist view meshed well with progressive social policies that encouraged universal education and universal suffrage. After all, according to this view, any child, whatever her economic condition or ethnic heritage, could be raised to succeed in life.

Sigmund Freud, as well, promoted the idea that experience, rather than physical differences, molded personality. Freud, however, concentrated on the lingering effects of early childhood experiences; thus, an adult might be anxious, fearful, or neurotic because of some traumatic experience or unresolved guilt. Freudians might view an aggressive little boy as furious at his mother for abandoning him, or jealous of his father for appropriating the affection of his mother.

Psychologists today argue about the validity of many of Freud's insights, but his contributions to our understanding of the role of the subconscious remain significant. Most modern psychologists agree that much of our emotional experience takes place in areas over which we have little conscious control. Whether we discuss this realm in terms of the id and ego, or refer to the anatomical structures of the brain's limbic system and the brain chemicals that regulate mood, we are acknowledging the fundamental role that emotion and feeling play in guiding our thoughts and our lives.

In the 1920s the Swiss psychologist Carl Jung outlined his view of the essential differences in human personality types in terms that are still useful. He described two basic types: the introvert, who by nature draws inward, away from the activity of the world; and the extrovert, who is outward-looking, and eager to act upon the physical world.

Jung's basic types were further broken down into subcategories based on how people perceive the world. Thus, both introverts and extroverts could approach life either emotionally or intellectually, intuitively or literally.

The correspondence is not precise, but Jung's introvert and extrovert are helpful descriptions of the two types of children examined in this series. The sensitive child has much in common with Jung's introvert; the demanding child described in this book shares much with Jung's extrovert. Her social skills may not be developed, so you may not think of her as being social and effectual, but her general thrust is outward and participatory. The demanding child does not spend life as a wallflower.

Psychological explanations of personality and temperament that stress early childhood experience over biologically determined traits can be liberating and uplifting. The implication is that any child has the potential to thrive, as long as the environment is nurturing and sound.

But there is a downside to those views as well. If a child does become deeply troubled—withdrawn, compulsive, aggressive or delinquent—it's easy to place "blame" on the environment. Emotional illness or personality difficulties may be attributed to inadequate parents—and usually the mother takes the brunt of this blame.

A new balance: biology reexamined

In the past few decades, our understanding of temperament has blossomed, in part because researchers have felt freer to examine biological explanations. At the same time, newly developed techniques for measuring behavior, tracking the actions of genes, and making images of the structure and activity of the brain have opened up exciting new avenues for research.

During this century, serious research into human behavior has focused on the interaction between biologically determined traits and the environment in which we grow: the time-honored balance between nature and nurture.

MEASURING TEMPERAMENT

Researchers who study temperament use a variety of techniques to make sure they are looking at innate temperament rather than behavior that is learned or influenced by a changing environment.

It's harder to observe and measure temperament as clearly and objectively as we do other innate qualities, like eye color or head shape. It's hard to say whether a particular child is aggressive or obstinate because of her genes, or because she has learned to fight for her rights.

So researchers observe the behavior of children in different situations to measure energy level, inhibition, willingness to approach, fearfulness, assertiveness, and other traits. The amount of time it takes a child to leave her mother's side in a new setting may be used as a measure of inhibition. The speed with which a child darts from one activity to another may track energy, activity level, or even the need for novelty and adventure. Some researchers have devised a "fidgetometer" to measure squirming in babies.

Psychologist and child development expert Jerome Kagan and his associates have conducted many of the studies that compare inhibited and uninhibited behaviors in children.

Kagan observed the behavior of fourteen-month-olds and their mothers in a playroom setting. Some of the children stuck close to their mothers and watched; others were drawn to a range of colorful toys and immediately began to play. When an unfamiliar adult entered the room and showed the children new toys, the inhibited children were wary and uncommunicative; the uninhibited children responded to this unfamiliar but interesting experience with enthusiasm.

The researchers also measured the children's heart rate, blood pressure, and saliva levels of cortisol, making a link between these behaviors and biological functions.

The children who were less inhibited—either happy, easy children or bold, demanding children—demonstrated their acceptance of stress in predictable ways: their blood pressure was lower, their heart rate didn't vary, and their levels of cortisol were lower.

Uninhibited children are not paralyzed by fear or shyness. They approach most new situations with zest and curiosity. Among those uninhibited children are the demanding children who are the subject of this book. These children, particularly those with impulsive and angry traits, behave with significantly *less* inhibition than most children.

TEMPERAMENT: ALL IN THE HEAD?

These observations of the behavior of children actually mesh with new discoveries in brain science. We now know a great deal about how brain chemicals known as neurotransmitters are produced and received, and how they are inhibited, transformed, or buffered by other chemicals. We know more about how medications can alter or improve mood. We know more about how these chemical patterns vary among individuals.

New evidence suggests that the particular mix of chemicals varies from person to person and may account, to an extent, for differences in temperament. For example, the neurotransmitter serotonin contributes to moods of well-being and satisfaction. Norepinephrine is associated with arousal and alertness, and, at higher levels, with anxiety.

People with low levels of serotonin are more likely to behave angrily and impulsively. Studies of prisoners show lower serotonin levels among those incarcerated for violent crimes; levels are lower among suicide victims as well. Similar findings suggest troubled children who behave aggressively and impulsively have lower levels of serotonin.

We've made great strides in understanding not only the chemistry of sensation and consciousness, but also the role of brain structure and function.

The limbic system—a cluster of structures deep within the brain—receives a stimulus and assigns a response and an emotional value: Is this stimulus pleasant? Unpleasant? Can it be ignored, or does it call for fighting or running away?

Often this assessment and response takes place before the thoughtful realm of the cerebrum has had a chance to evaluate the stimulus rationally. Thus we see a snake and instantly recoil before the higher brain processes the evidence and informs us that what we see is actually the coiled garden hose.

There is still much to be learned about how different temperaments relate to brain structure and function. But there is evidence that people who consistently are restless and energetic, have a high pain threshold, are outgoing, and are easily bored may have a biological basis for their personality traits.

Most likely this biological basis is centered in the degree of excitability of the limbic system. These structures control those basic responses and emotions we share with lower animals: fear, anger, alertness, sexual desire. The hippocampus, for example, distinguishes between familiar and unfamiliar stimuli and plays a role in the memory of emotions. If it detects an unfamiliar, or unpleasant, stimulus, it stimulates the nearby amygdala, a small structure that regulates the fear response.

The limbic system also performs the crucial function of regulating "response inhibition," the slowing and modifying of impulses. If there is damage or abnormality in these regions, the effect is to increase impulsivity. Other abnormalities can result in what's called "perseverative behavior," the tendency to repeat behavior whether it's rewarded or not.

Not all this variation is abnormal. Healthy people vary in both response inhibition and perseverative behavior, and those normal variations are what this book is about.

Research with animals suggests that when the brain has more connections between the emotional centers of the limbic system and the parts of the brain that control movement, emotional stimuli are more readily translated into physical action.

A child who is energetic and physically impulsive might well possess a brain that has more neural pathways between the limbic system and the parts of the brain that control movement.

A child who is physically brave and seems to laugh off threats and punishments may be blessed with lower levels of norepinephrine.

In addition to these tendencies, each child has her own rhythm of arousal and relaxation. For example, a sensitive, reactive child has quick responses, becomes anxious and alert quickly, and takes longer to calm down after a threatening or unfamiliar experience.

But a bold, outgoing child may seek novelty because she recovers, neurologically speaking, more quickly from novel experiences. Her hippocampus and amygdala are less excitable, and prepare her to take on additional stimuli more quickly.

TEMPERAMENT AND GENES

Most definitions of temperament include the element of heritability. They assume a genetic basis for human variation in behavior, but evidence is difficult to come by. No one has yet identified a "noisy gene," or a "tantrum gene," or a "can't-sit-still gene." We can't track and identify these traits by selectively breeding humans for certain qualities, the way we do with dogs.

One approach is to sort out genetic from environmental influences by studying twins, who offer a unique window into the workings of biology and environment.

Several studies have examined groups of twins, observed their behavior and temperament, and then compared the way sets of identical twins differ from pairs of fraternal twins. This distinction is key to studying how much of a trait may be explained by genes.

Identical, or monozygotic, twins come from one egg that divides after fertilization, and thus they share the same genetic material. Fraternal, or dizygotic, twins are the result of the fertilization of two eggs by two sperm. Thus, although they share the same intrauterine environment and the same birthday, fraternal twins are no more alike than any other two siblings.

In twin studies of behavior, researchers observe groups of identical twins and compare their behavior to groups of fraternal twins. Since all identical twins are same-sex, they are matched with same-sex fraternal twin pairs in these studies.

These experiments also control for environmental influences by studying twin pairs who are being raised together in normal families, so each child has essentially the same life experiences as the other. If the identical twin pairs show more similarity to each other than the fraternal twins do, the differences are very likely genetic.

These studies do not point to a particular gene, or easily identified genetic trait that produces the qualities of the demanding child. They do suggest, however, that the entire spectrum of biological traits has combined to provide a child with a predisposition toward these behaviors.

However, the most recent work in behavioral genetics is suggesting some fascinating links. Two studies, one conducted at Herzog Memorial Hospital in Jerusalem and another at the National Institutes of Mental Health in Washington, reported similar conclusions in early 1996: A particular gene seems clearly linked to a particular personality trait that's found in normal people.

The gene, called D4DR, appears to determine how receptive brain cells are to the enzyme dopamine, a brain chemical associated with feelings of excitement, energy, and arousal. It is found in two forms: one with a longer sequence of DNA in one segment, and the other with shorter.

Subjects with the longer sequence ranked at the top of a scale of "novelty-seeking" behavior. Novelty seekers are normal but tend to enjoy and seek out excitement and change in their lives. They're the people who take risks, make dramatic career changes or blast off in space shuttles.

The majority of the people in the study had the shorter sequence, and scored about average for risk-taking and novelty-seeking.

It's certainly possible that as more is learned about the specific genes that guide the production and function of brain chemicals, we will see more evidence of genetic explanations for many of the behaviors we observe among demanding children.

Of course, even when the hereditary explanation of a particular behavior is strong, it is never total. There is still a significant part of any child's temperament that has explanations other than genetics, and that is the realm of environment, early childhood experience, and the wisdom and skills of parents.

TEMPERAMENT AND SURVIVAL

If temperament has a genetic basis, it must have some survival value. It's easy to imagine how demanding traits could contribute to survival. A bold, aggressive, forceful temperament had value in prehistoric times, especially in the effort to hunt for food and vanquish enemies. And a trait like adaptability—the ability to adjust to new situations or even to seek out and embrace the unfamiliar—certainly could contribute to survival.

Impulsivity may not be a trait we celebrate when we have to take a child into a china store. But daring and courage and the ability to spring into action have had their value throughout human history.

Anger, also, has its uses in warning off enemies or rousing us and others to action.

And persistence pays off in innumerable ways. It gives us the ability to stick to a difficult task. It makes us less likely to become discouraged when the going gets tough, and it makes us unsatisfied with second-best.

TEMPERAMENT IS NOT DESTINY

As intriguing as the biological discoveries about temperament may be, they still are only part of the story. If we put too much emphasis on either biology or environment, we run the risk of overlooking the subtle, complex ways these realms interact with each other.

If we overemphasize biological explanations, we may tend to view our children's personalities fatalistically, to assume that temperament is destiny and beyond our influence as parents. And that view might prevent us from helping our children broaden their skills, their abilities, and their confidence.

If, on the other hand, we ignore the biological roots of temperament, attributing all aspects of personality to environment, we may be tempted to try to change or "cure" qualities that are innate, qualities that have inherent worth.

And if our children disappoint us or develop problems, we as parents can become burdened with guilt, agonizing over what we might have done to cause our child to push another pre-schooler off the swing.

Ultimately, however, biology and environmental influence are so closely woven together that it's exceedingly difficult to sort them out. We vary in the minute details of how our brains are "wired," in our production of chemicals that either promote or inhibit a feeling or an action. Yet these details are not the totality of personality. They form a framework on which to hang our unique life experiences.

If a child is born with a tendency toward impulsive behavior, and is born into a family that sets few limits on her behavior, her wildness will probably be reinforced.

If this child acts out her aggressive behavior by hitting and bullying other children without external restraints, her behavior will drive her peers away. That rejection will further weaken her sense of self-worth, and quite possibly increase her angry behavior.

It appears that the brain continues to forge attachments and connections throughout life as experiences are repeated. Neurons build pathways and reinforce them with additional connections. So even if every human brain is, at birth, unique in its general predisposition toward excitability or need for novelty, that brain also accumulates a unique history of experience that builds and shapes it.

The basic tendencies may persist, but the brain is not limited to, or captive to, those tendencies.

The totality of the influence of nature and nurture on personality has been described as a gray fabric, with the black threads of the warp representing the biological underpinnings, and the white weft threads representing the experience built upon it. The fabric as a whole is neither white nor black but gray.

Your child's temperament is really a bias toward certain kinds of behavior. She will be more comfortable in certain settings than others, and learn certain behaviors and habits more easily.

Genes can affect our behavior in roundabout ways. Certain temperaments may lead us to select certain environments; we may gravitate toward realms in which we feel temperamentally comfortable, thus reinforcing the original tendencies. So your child may find it hard to sit still or to control her temper, and gravitate toward high-energy recreations and amusements. She may prefer dance lessons and soccer to reading, and those activities will reinforce her tendency to be active and outgoing.

But that doesn't mean that she'll never be able to sit at a desk and do her schoolwork, or that she can't learn to manage her temper.

What's crucial is how her family brings her up, praises her, sets limits, prepares her for difficult situations, and talks to her about her weaknesses and her strengths.

The link between nature and nurture is complex and circular. And the conclusion must be that despite the fundamental importance of temperament, it is *not* destiny. Rather, it is a bias toward certain behaviors, a style of behavior that feels right to a particular child. It is not fate, and neither is it an assemblage of superficial habits and quirks. Rather, it is a birthright.

◆ 3 ◇

The Challenge: Why Raising a Demanding Child Is So . . . Demanding!

"One of the hardest things for me to deal with," says one mother of a demanding child, "is The Look. When we're shopping or doing errands, Brandon gets overstimulated and sometimes gets out of control. When I tell him to calm down or refuse to get him something he wants, he loses it and throws a tantrum.

"In stores, I can see the other shoppers watching, and then they give me an exasperated, eye-rolling look. I'm very familiar with The Look, because I'm sorry to say I used to give it to other parents before I had kids."

Having your child misbehave in public certainly can be embarrassing. But the challenge of raising a child who is difficult, impulsive, or explosive goes beyond an occasional red face.

In this chapter, we'll examine what it is about demanding children that take a toll on parents—especially if the parents do not manage to get the support and help they need in learning to manage their child's temperament.

• **Guilt**. When we feel we are not being good parents, when we doubt our effectiveness, we feel that we've failed in a role that means more to us than any other. As Nick's mother said in the opening chapter of this book, "I used to be a good mother." Demanding children can turn the best parents into inadequate ones—or ones who feel inadequate. Often it's the most conscientious parents, the ones with the highest expectations for themselves and the highest hopes for their children, who feel inadequate and betrayed.

In addition, we may suffer from the concern that our child's temperament is our fault, that our child is demanding because of something we did wrong.

• **Envy**. "I find myself envying parents who have quiet, sedate children," says one mother. "I watch these kids sit still at a restaurant, reaching for the salt or the ketchup so slowly and carefully, not spilling anyone's coffee, keeping their clothes clean. I think, 'I'd be a great Mom if I had kids like that!' Sometimes they look at the ruckus over at our table, and I think, 'Look, lady, you wouldn't be so smug if you had *my* kids at your table!'"

• **Resentment**. When our demanding children are giving us a particularly bad time, we feel put-upon and resentful. We start feeing sorry for ourselves, and feel less empathy with what might be bothering our child or contributing to his behavior.

"He knows how to push all my buttons," observes a mother. "I've been really preoccupied recently because my father-in-law is in the hospital, and both my husband and I have a lot on our minds. But does David care? No—he picks this week to be worse than ever."

"My son's behavior is wearing me out. From the time he comes in the door after school until he finally goes to sleep at night, my nerves are on edge. It's one constant battle over everything from his homework to television to getting him to put his dishes in the dishwasher."

• **Anger**. Impulsive, energetic kids who break their toys, snap their shoelaces every time they tie them, or gallop across newly seeded lawns despite our warnings can cause our patience to snap. When our children lose their tempers, we often lose our own. And when children pick and whine and nag and won't let us alone when we're tired, our annoyance sometimes turns into rage. And then we have to cope with our child's demanding traits and our own anger as well. We'll discuss anger—in child and in parent—in Chapter 7.

• **More guilt**. We feel ashamed of our resentment, our impatience and our anger. As one mother puts it, "When he's good, I feel guilty for how mad I was at him when he was bad!"

• **Anxiety**. We worry about our child's happiness, his future, his very survival. "Jessica is so defiant, so resistant to following rules. She seems determined to do the opposite of what I want and what's best for her. Last night I woke up at two a.m. in a cold sweat with this terrible realization: In three years, she's going to be a teenager! *Then* what?"

SOMETIMES I'M UP, SOMETIMES I'M DOWN

One of the core difficulties of being the parent of a demanding child is finding and keeping an emotional even keel.

Parents of demanding children report extreme mood swings in terms of their feelings and attitudes toward their children. It's almost like a Dr. Jekyll–Mr. Hyde situation, in which you alternate between being a loving, patient, confident parent, and an insecure, exasperated scold.

"As a parent, I often feel I'm on a seesaw," said the mother of a nine-year-old demanding child. "The highs and lows are so extreme. Sometimes I want to throw him out the window. Other times I'm so touched by his kindness, or his generosity, and I just couldn't love him more. And then I feel so guilty about the negative feelings I had."

You alternate between wanting to hug him one day and wanting to strangle him the next.

You alternate between resenting him, and all the stress he brings you one day, and feeling ashamed of your resentment the next.

One day you feel overcontrolling, overly strict, overly rigid and inflexible. The next day you feel you're too lax, and your child is out of control and taking advantage of you.

"It's so hard for us to figure Alexa out. She's so resistant to any limits we set. When she misbehaves, we restrict her and take away more and more privileges. It gets to the point that we feel like monsters, so the next day, we relax and go easy on her. Sometimes it seems that she's in charge, not us."

These ups and down of emotion can be disconcerting, to say the least. But they can also result in serious inconsistencies of discipline and limit setting: You're firm and unyielding one day, vague and forgiving the next.

Your varied feelings about your child may continue, but you will be more effective as a parent if you understand and accept them as a normal aspect of the job. Recognizing that they come with the territory of demanding children is a first step in easing their power over you.

BEWARE OF BURNOUT

But there's another difficulty that comes with raising a child who is unusually impulsive, relentless, explosive. It's a problem that's so obvious it's often overlooked. It's called fatigue.

Being a parent is tiring and time-consuming under the best of circumstances. When your child is a newborn, you manage to live on minimal sleep. You spend your child's toddler years at a constant gallop. You devote all your energy and attention to your child's well-being and happiness.

But a demanding child takes even more of a toll on parental energy resources. This is especially true of the high-energy child, who goes on and on like the Energizer Bunny. And the impulsive child seems bent on getting into trouble or injuring himself without constant supervision. Both the persistent child and the angry child drain us of energy more quickly than more easygoing children.

Demanding children also bring with them emotional stress that can be more depleting than physical exhaustion.

A major reason for the emotional battering parents of demanding children take is the reduced sense of reward. With easier children, all the sacrifices and stresses are worth it because there's an enormous payoff. Your newborn pays you back for all those sleepless nights with a smile that melts your heart. After driving you to your wits' end all weekend, your three-year-old rewards you with a scribbled Valentine. And then the ordinary sacrifices seem more than worth it.

We often don't recognize the extent to which we need to get some reinforcement, some reward from all our parenting efforts. Because demanding children don't always provide those rewards, we become emotionally drained. The result: burnout.

And what happens when parents reach the end of their rope? They run the risk of emotional withdrawal. They retreat from interaction with their children, often just when their children most need their help. At the very least, the resources and strengths they bring to parenting are depleted.

The following symptoms are signs that your struggle to do right by your own demanding child may be taking too big a toll:

• **Fatigue**. Just as with the first months of an infant's life, life with a demanding child can be physically exhausting. But unlike the newborn, the demanding child's behavior continues, and his Terrible Twos stage turns into the Threatening Threes and the Ferocious Fours. If you aren't getting enough rest, if you're feeling run-down keeping up with your child, you are risking burnout.

• **Isolation**. Demanding children sometimes become isolated from their peers when their behavior is annoying or disruptive. Similarly, parents can become isolated as well from the camaraderie of playground parents. And if the child's behavior is humiliating or worrisome to the parents, they may be afraid to reach out to others, because they'd have to admit their weaknesses and failures. In so doing, they end up denying themselves the support they need.

• **Shorter tempers, shorter fuses**. A reduced ability to tolerate the ordinary frustrations of parenthood usually signals that fatigue and stress have gotten out of hand.

• **Loss of sense of pleasure and fun**. When family life is stressful, there's less opportunity for the pleasures that bind families together. It's hard to enjoy life or even to plan pleasurable activities like vacations and outings when everyone is on edge. If there's less laughter in your home than there used to be, you may be on the road to burnout.

• **The sense of being trapped**. Sometimes parents feel incapable of being effective parents but feel they have no one to turn to for support. And they may be afraid to open up to others about their concerns, keeping their child's troubles to themselves. Or they feel they're the only person in the world who understands their child. Who else loves him as they do? Who else will see past the difficult behavior to appreciate his inner virtues?

• **Fantasies of escape.** It's natural to yearn for a trip to the Caribbean during a difficult spell of parenthood. But parents on the brink of burnout may spend more time harboring fantasies of getting away from it all—and then feel even more guilty.

When a pattern of burnout or pre-burnout symptoms emerges, it's time to call in reinforcements; it's time to reach out. That's what you're doing, reading this book. The techniques and insights presented in this book are designed to provide parents of demanding children with the support and relief they need—and deserve.

WHERE DID WE GO WRONG?

Parents of demanding children face many challenges that are essentially practical, such as how to set reasonable limits, cope with tantrums, or encourage cooperative play. These are issues that we'll address in Chapter 6. But that's only half the battle. Demanding children take a toll on parents, provoke worries and anxieties, and call into question parents' sense of competence and worthiness.

Questions that often arise include:

- What makes my child tick? Why does he *do* those things?
- Why is he so different from me?
- Have I failed my child? What did I do wrong? Did I do something wrong to make him so angry, so hostile? Was I too strict, too lenient?
- Did I go back to work too soon? Should I have breast-fed?
- How can I meet the needs of my challenging child and still do right by my other children who don't ask so much of me?
- What's going to become of my demanding child when he grows up? Will he ever learn to share? Will he alienate everyone on the playground? Will he punch his boss in the nose?
- Even when I understand my child, how do I explain him to other people who don't? How do I stand up for my child in a constructive way? How can I get others to recognize the lovable child I know is in there?

DEMANDING BEHAVIOR AND YOUR OWN HISTORY

No matter what our own temperament might be, the challenging behaviors described in this book are familiar to all of us because we've all had to deal with them. We may possess these traits ourselves. Or we may have grown up with parents, siblings, or other relatives who have these challenging tendencies. We may have struggled to cope with playmates, teachers, lovers, co-workers, and neighbors who were impulsive, fidgety, or hostile.

Whatever our exposure, our experience with demanding people has generated a complex web of attitudes and expectations. It's wise to take a moment and review our own memories and feelings toward demanding behavior before we get busy with the task of helping our own children.

Which of the following statements strike a chord in your memory?

1. I was pretty rambunctious as a kid and I got soundly punished for it.
2. My older brother was a terror. If I bothered him in any way, he'd go into a rage and break things. I learned to be very careful around him because his anger terrified me.
3. My little sister used to follow me around and nag me until I couldn't stand it. If I got mad at her or complained to my parents, they took her side.
4. I wasn't allowed to run all over a restaurant and bother the other diners, and I don't think kids today should.
5. I was really wild as a teenager. I did things without thinking, including driving my dad's car into a tree. I shudder to think of my child taking the risks I took.
6. I never had trouble making friends, but I had trouble keeping them because of my hair-trigger temper. I want my child to cope with anger better than I did.
7. I was taught to feel disapproval toward parents

who wouldn't or couldn't control their children. Now I can't control mine!

8. My father used to go into terrible rages when I misbehaved. I was terrified of his anger, and to this day, I can't think clearly when someone expresses anger like that.

9. My parents were too strict, and I'm determined not to repeat their mistakes.

10. My parents let me get away with murder, and I'm determined not to repeat their mistakes.

The questions that you're able to answer in the affirmative can draw your attention to particular areas that may complicate your relationship with your challenging child. If your childhood was full of frightening experiences with anger, for example, that will affect how you respond when your own child becomes angry—or you become angry at him.

Your own past and your own attitudes both contribute to your parental philosophy and style. You'll be able to focus your energies more effectively if you can learn to separate your uncomfortable memories from your child's behavior in the present.

HOW YOUR TEMPERAMENT INTERACTS WITH YOUR CHILD'S

Just as children are born with different temperaments, so were their parents. Despite the degree of genetic foundation for temperament, children do not necessarily have the same temperament as their parents, any more than they have the same color hair or the same talent for art, music, or gymnastics.

If you've identified your child's style of demanding behavior, you've probably given some thought to what your own temperament is and how it meshes with your child's. If you're a demanding adult, you've probably recognized yourself, as well as your child, in these pages. (If you're shy, introverted, or cautious by nature, take a look at *The Sensitive Child* volume for descriptions and see if you recognize yourself there.)

The drawback of similar temperaments is that parents may not be able to help expand their child's skills. It isn't enough for the child to be happy and comfortable; he needs to broaden his abilities as well. No matter how comfortable the child is in his home situation, he needs to be prepared to get along in the outside world.

And it's when parent and child are very much alike that it's sometimes hardest for parents to let go of their own burden of childhood memories. If the child is heading for the same kind of trouble the parent remembers and perhaps regrets, the parent may overreact or become overly anxious about the child's well-being.

When parent and child have decidedly different temperaments, the mix can be positive if the parent's temperament helps modify the child's excesses (or vice versa). An intense, easily angered child may thrive with parents who are patient and calm.

But often, when temperaments don't mesh, when parent and child seem to be at one another's throats in everything they do, parents can be baffled and disappointed. In these situations parents can, despite the best of intentions, actually hinder their child's progress (more on this in Chapter 5).

But ultimately, any combination of temperaments has the potential to work well for the child, because a good rapport, or "fit," is forged in each family.

Let's look at the demanding traits described in Chapter 1 and see how the mixes or matches of temperament can play out in family relationships.

THE HIGH-ENERGY CHILD

If your high-energy child lives in a family full of energetic, busy, on-the-go people, that's a pretty good fit. True, the furniture may suffer, and the cat may hide under the bed when the whole family gets together and fills the house with noise and exuberance. But emotionally the family is on the same wavelength.

However, that does not mean that a high-energy child needs no guidance. He still needs to learn to accommodate to social expectations. He won't be able to bounce on everybody's sofa, and he'll benefit from learning to modulate his voice and noise levels. He'll have to get used to sitting still some of the time and working quietly some of the time.

But it's a different story altogether when the child is high-energy and the parents are not. The normal disconnect between child and adult energy levels is even worse. To a quiet, introverted parent, an excess of action and noise is stressful and can feel threatening. The result is that the parent can easily grow to resent the energetic child.

"I find myself yelling at Colin just for being Colin," said one. "I can step back some of the time and think, 'He doesn't mean anything by it. He's just a kid, and that's just the way he is.' But other times, I just can't stand the noise, and I get extremely impatient."

The fact is, Colin and other demanding children will have to make some adjustments, too. As they mature, they'll need to learn that the world will expect some moderation of their temperament. And introverted parents may be better able to interpret those expectations and help a high-energy child adjust to them.

THE IMPULSIVE CHILD

When both parent and child are impulsive, the fit can be quite good. As with the high-energy child, the impulsive child who grows up in a relaxed, spontaneous family feels in synch with his surroundings.

"We're both the same," says the mother of an impulsive daughter. "We both like to act. We hate planning and anticipating."

The danger of this mix is that the child may not have enough impetus to learn self-control. A cautious parent can protect her impulsive child and help him stay out of danger. When both parent and child are impulsive, the challenge is to help the child learn self-control and learn to take responsibility for his own well-being.

When the child is impulsive and the parents are cautious, the mix can be frustrating for the child and terrifying for the parents.

"When Matt was four, we stopped at a motel that had a swimming pool," recalled Matt's father. "He had never been in water deeper than a wading pool before. We went to the pool, and were just putting our towels down when Matt slipped into the water and stood there on the bottom, totally submerged. When we scooped him out, he wasn't even upset.

"I can't anticipate the crazy stuff he'll do, so I feel helpless to warn him. I'm always berating him for the risks he took, when it's too late."

It's not just the child's fearlessness that's hard on cautious parents.

"I always take my time before making decisions," says a mother. "Sometimes, when I've had to make a decision under pressure, I've made a bad choice. My son never thinks about anything before he acts. I worry that he's going to make decisions he regrets."

THE ANGRY CHILD

The angry child who grows up in a family where emotions come to a boil easily can have a difficult time, because anger tends to feed on itself.

"We're both short-tempered," says one mother of her nine-year-old son. "When he tests me too much, I blow up. That doesn't help. Sometimes I think he'd be better with a mom who's calm, someone who would respond to him by saying very gently, 'Now Kyle. . . . '"

"I'm incapable of hiding it when I'm upset," said another mother. "I try to stay calm as long as I can, but I'm like a stick of dynamite and he's lit the end. It's just a matter of time."

The angry child in an intense family has the advantage of belonging. But even when the similar temperaments generate an atmosphere of tolerance and acceptance of expressions of intense emotion, a demanding child needs help learning to cope with and manage anger. More and more, the culture at large will reward people who are capable of cooperating with others and managing conflict constructively. Your demanding child needs to learn ways to get along in that milieu, even if the family situation is tolerant.

When the angry child has parents who don't share that temperament, he may not have appropriate limits placed on his behavior. His parents may be baffled and upset by his outburst, and may be too accommodating and unable to stand up to him.

Sooner or later, these parents do usually blow their stack, and then feel uncomfortable with their own reaction.

"My child has a terrible temper," says one such mother. "When he's denied something he wants or when we have to make him do something he doesn't want to do, he loses control. Normally, I'm fairly calm. I don't fly off the handle much. But when Brad gets going, he gets ME so upset that I get angry. Then we make quite a pair!''

THE PERSISTENT CHILD

Some persistent kids are very sociable. They can't get enough personal interaction. If you and your child have the same appetite for giving and receiving attention, the mix can be quite good.

However, other persistent traits can generate problems when both parent and child share temperament. Persistent children, for example, get locked into unproductive behavior. They might complain endlessly about something that happened at school, even though the event is over and done with. Often they'll make unreasonable demands, and stick to them despite parental refusals. If their parents have a similar temperament, it's easy to get into a situation in which both parent and child are being stubborn, and the situation ends up in gridlock.

''My daughter and I are both stubborn,'' says one mother. ''When she was little, we used to have terrible battles over food. I'd insist that she eat her meat, and she would absolutely refuse, and it went on and on. It's always been very hard for either of us to back down.''

Parents who don't share persistence with their child often feel threatened and invaded by their child's seemingly endless need for attention. An introverted parent and a persistent child can result in parental exhaustion and impatience, as the intrusive child constantly invades the parent's carefully guarded space. Naturally, this feeling dampens the positive feelings parents want to have toward their child.

It can be difficult for parents to sympathize with a persistent child who can't let go of her unhappiness. Caitlin is particularly concerned with issues of injustice—in particular, injustice against *her*. When she tells her parents about her school day, she delivers a precise litany of how so-and-so hurt her feelings, and the teacher wasn't fair, and nobody likes her.

Caitlin's mother tries to be patient, but she finds herself issuing dismissive denials. "Oh, it wasn't that bad," she'll say, or "I'm sure she didn't mean it."

Parents of persistent, insatiable children are often baffled by the child's inability to limit himself. They give more time, attention, praise, cookies, presents. But nothing is enough.

"Our older daughter, Whitney, would sometimes whine when she wanted something," said the father of two daughters. "We handled that easily by ignoring her until she found a better way to tell us what she needed. But with Elizabeth, the whines just go on and on and on. She gets louder and louder and never stops."

In child development circles, the term "fit" is not limited to the degree to which parent and child temperaments match. Parents and children often differ, and yet manage well. What is usually referred to is the relationship that parent and child build, a workable and livable fit between parental expectations and the child's abilities. And that, ultimately, is what you, as the parent of a demanding child, will be working toward. Whatever the match or mismatch between your temperament and that of your child, you can create a fit and rapport that works.

Whether our own temperaments are demanding or sensitive, daring or cautious, extrovert or introvert, we all share the desire to see our children grow up happy. Sometimes that means we want them to enjoy what *we* enjoyed as children, other times to be spared what we suffered as kids.

The key to raising your child is to empathize, but to empathize *appropriately*. That means that if you suffered from your difficult temperament and see the same tendencies in your child, you need to respond to your child's experiences in an adult way, rather than as the hurt child you remember being.

FIT AND OTHERS

The issue of fit applies to many dimensions of your child's life, and not just in your relationship to him. A poor temperament fit between your demanding child and his brothers and sisters, for example, can make issues like family routines and discipline into major problems.

The same problems can occur with your child's relationship with other family members.

"My son is highly energetic, and has a hard time sitting still. We've managed at home by childproofing the house and giving him lots of space to play outside. The problem is my in-laws. They're very quiet, cautious people. They love Justin, but when he's active, they act as if they'd never seen a child before. The chemistry between them and my son is not positive. I'm always warning him before we see them, not to touch, not to make too much noise."

Relatives sometimes compound these problems by comparing children within a family, and by being critical or judgmental about the parents' skills. All of this naturally adds to parental stress.

The same problems of fit are possible between your child and his teacher, camp counselor, coach, or—later in life—boss, neighbor, or co-worker. We all have to learn how to get along with others who differ from us, or who rub us the wrong way (or whom we rub the wrong way). As your demanding child matures, and with your help, he will gradually learn ways to establish a better fit with others.

We discuss issues of fit as they relate to specific settings and situations in Chapter 8.

FIT AS A TWO-WAY STREET

Your child's temperament can influence your behavior as a parent, just as your own personality and behavior influence your child. Parents certainly teach their children, but children teach parents and other adults, too. We are not fated to remain locked into a temperament dynamic that isn't working, whether it's different temperaments that don't mesh well, or identical temperaments that don't allow enough growth. What parents can do is learn to understand their child's temperament and adjust their parenting style to accommodate it.

Your demanding child's temperament has helped form the kind of parent you are. If your child is challenging, the chances are that it's not your "fault"; rather, it's probably a combination of his temperament, your own, and the specifics of your child-management approach. You can't do much about temperament, but you can find better ways to manage the challenging aspects of temperament.

While it's difficult to raise a demanding child, it's also challenging to *be* one. Parents who understand the challenges their child is facing will be better able to establish rapport. We'll discuss what it feels like to be a demanding child in Chapter 4.

◇ 4 ◇

A View from the Inside: What Your Demanding Child Experiences

"Last night I was helping Andrew with his homework. He was studying for a test, and we were in in his room going over a list of terms he had to memorize for social studies. He was lying on the floor, absolutely writhing. I was snapping at him, telling him to calm down and concentrate on his work.

"Finally I realized that he really was memorizing those words. I'd ask him a word, and he'd squirm and thrash for a while and then he'd remember the answer. He actually remembers better when he's wiggling."

Andrew is a high-energy fifth-grader whose body tells him that it *has* to move. As he puts it, "I can't concentrate when I have to sit still. It takes so much energy to keep all the parts of me still that I can't think!"

The world of demanding children is full of people like Andrew who pace and fidget and always have to be doing two things at once. They grow up to be the adults who can't talk on the phone unless they're walking around or can't drive without fiddling with sunglasses and radio dials.

They become the people who plunge "cold" into new situations, think on their feet, seek out new challenges, and improvise as they go along.

They become adults whose passions and sense of justice are easily aroused, who feel their faces flush and their temperatures rise when fate treats them or others unfairly.

They become adults who pursue their goals singlemindedly and don't give up when the going gets rough.

Too often, the behavior of the demanding child is defined by people on the outside looking in. The outsider sees aggression, while the angry child sees herself as standing up for her rights. The outsider sees nagging, when the persistent child sees herself as trying valiantly to get her needs met.

As the parent of a demanding child, you need to "try on" her temperament, to go beyond what it looks like to you, and gain an understanding of what it feels like to her.

This empathy is especially important if you and your child have dramatically different temperaments. If you are naturally calm and quiet, it may take an effort to understand your child's need to be busy and active.

If you can accomplish this, you will be less likely to misdiagnose your child's behavior. Your task is to understand your child's temperament, and to help her define it in positive terms and manage its challenging aspects.

And until these tasks are accomplished, parents run the risk of misunderstanding their children, misinterpreting their behavior, and missing opportunities for helping their children grow and thrive.

WHAT HAPPENS WHEN YOU FAIL TO "TRY ON" HER TEMPERAMENT

• You misdiagnose your child's behavior. You say she is being defiant when she's desperate. You say she's being lazy when she's preoccupied. You say she's whining when she's trying to get help easing her discomfort.

• You develop a victim mentality. You begin to talk yourself into powerless parenting behavior. "Whatever I do, it's wrong. No matter what I try, I can't seem to get her to (do her homework, sit still, give me a moment's peace). She's just doing this to make me miserable."

• You deny her real perceptions. "You've had enough time to play with Katrina," you might say. "Now you're tired and you need to come in for some rest." But your child knows what she feels. Perhaps she isn't the least bit tired. She is entitled to her own perceptions, even if they're different from yours.

• You run the risk of making your child's core identity into a negative:

"I can't understand why you have to grab everything!"

"Why do you always take everything personally?"

"Do you have to be so stubborn?"

"Oh, quit whining."

• You are less successful as her advocate if you are unable to understand what lies behind her difficult behavior and explain it to others.

• You miss the opportunities for intimacy that come from understanding your child fully.

DEMANDING BEHAVIOR FROM THE INSIDE

Demanding children are not always able to articulate their feelings, especially when they are very young. But your child will convey through her actions and her body language what's going on inside. Certainly the toddler who screams and throws her toys is conveying her anger quite eloquently.

As your child grows older, and with your help, she'll develop the language she needs to explain her feelings to you. The more your child is able to articulate her feelings and teach you how she reacts to specific situations, the more you'll be able to develop empathy with her. Let's see how each category of demanding behavior feels to the child experiencing it:

THE HIGH-ENERGY CHILD

Here's how a second-grade teacher describes her highly energetic pupils:

"You can just see how hard it is. It's brutal for them. They can't sit still. When it's time to work, they're masters of avoidance. They go to the bathroom, then they sharpen their pencil forty-two times. They have to touch, have to say something. They're supposed to sit and focus, but they just can't."

The high-energy child needs to move. Sitting still is as tiring for her as a few hours of tap dancing might be for a more sedate person. When your high-energy child is being restricted—in the classroom, or in the car, or anywhere that movement is discouraged or forbidden, she feels trapped. Her stress builds up, and she feel more urgency in her need to release tension.

If you are a calm, introverted parent of a high-energy child, try to imagine the way you feel when your child and her friends are wild and out of control. You are supposed to be in charge of them, but you feel under pressure and powerless to keep them from hurting themselves or one another. That's how your child feels inside when she can't move and release tension. She's supposed to be in control of her body, but it just isn't happening.

High-energy children often do things without being conscious of doing them. Their fingers have little minds of their own, picking at the edges of the wallpaper until a strip peels off, or repeatedly bending a toy until it breaks.

Often the energetic child sees limits as a form of rejection. Rules and fences and timetables that seem perfectly reasonable to adults seem like personal affronts to her. Certainly, she runs up against enough limits during her busy day. It's difficult for her to see the logic to those limits, even though they may be there for her own safety.

THE IMPULSIVE CHILD

Like high-energy children, impulsive kids often blunder into trouble and are reprimanded for actions they weren't entirely aware of. Before they know it, they're in trouble because something mysteriously got broken or eaten, or somebody got waked up at dawn or punched in the nose.

This disconnection between what the child intended and what she ended up actually doing can lead to a sense of fatalism. Things just "happen" to the impulsive child. It's hard for her to develop a sense of empowerment, of cause-and-effect. After all, when the effect comes so instantly after the cause, there's little sense of consequence, and little motivation to control or plan her actions.

But the impulsive child senses that she didn't commit these acts with hostile intent. When she says, "I didn't mean to!" she's telling the truth. And she feels bad that people are always mad at her for things she didn't mean to do.

THE ANGRY CHILD

We all know what anger feels like. Our muscles tense, our skin flushes, our teeth grit. We feel our temperature rise, our internal pressures mounting.

Those pressures urge us toward action.

As adults, we have years of experience with the consequences of our own anger. We may remember being punished for having a tantrum as children, or getting in trouble for breaking things or pummeling our brothers and sisters. Over time, we learned to gain some control over our intense emotions and how we acted on them.

Your child, however, has limited experience and limited skills. So for her, the many frustrations that childhood brings are translated quickly into rage.

For a child, the world is full of frustrations, from the "No!" issued to the toddler, to the demands of school, the restrictions on where and how long to play. Childhood is full of rules and limits. There's all the injustice of big brothers who get to stay up later, classmates who taunt, and playmates who cheat at checkers.

Then there's the physical world of zippers that don't zip and pencils that break and math books that get left in school lockers.

The actual events that provoke anger may seem trivial, but the intensity of childhood anger is not.

Anger prompts a rush of adrenaline-related hormones that urge us to act. Yet one of the ironies of anger is that when we yield to the impulse by screaming, lashing out or breaking something, we often feel *worse*, not better.

So your child may have a tantrum, but not really feel better afterward. That's especially true if the injustice or frustration that prompted it remains.

For some children, anger is a response not so much to frustration, but to a perceived threat to status or self-esteem. Some children respond to criticism from adults or teasing by classmates with hurt feelings and tears. Other children respond to these same situations with rage. Sometimes the impetus seems minor: Being teased, failing to come in first in the race, or being told to copy a school assignment more neatly—a seemingly ordinary event can become the trigger for an angry outburst.

Children who are angry and defiant often sense their own power and how difficult it is to control. It's scary to be unable to restrain all that power, or to have parents who seem unable to control it. The angry child needs limits, and will ultimately feel safer, despite her protests.

For some children (and adults), however, anger is energizing and stimulating. If circumstances don't make them angry, they'll provoke anger all by themselves because it feels good.

"Every once in a while, my son decides to get mad at me. Out of the blue, he'll ask for something he knows he can't have, just to hear me say no. Then he'll up the ante, asking for more things, knowing I'll say no, and then he can be mad. Finally he's worked himself into a fury of victimhood—over nothing!"

Angry children often orchestrate situations that seem designed to provoke anger—and provide an excuse for the child's expression of anger. The child pokes and pokes. When the parent finally becomes angry, the child feels relieved.

When that need to provoke or express anger is denied, the situation can become explosive indeed.

Take Brad, who likes to signal his displeasure by

slamming doors behind him. He often leaves for school on an angry note, slamming the door decisively behind him. One weekend, Brad's father bought a new, energy-efficient door with special weather stripping. The new door didn't slam; it closed with a softer resistance. On Monday morning, Brad stormed out the door. No slam! He returned and tried again. Still no slam. When his ritual display of anger was thwarted, his anger became real.

THE PERSISTENT CHILD

When Alex was three, his parents fenced in their backyard so he'd have a safe place to play. Until then, Alex had enjoyed his small swing set, his sandbox, and the green lawn under the trees.

But once the chain-link fence went up, Alex was miserable. He no longer played in the sandbox or on the swing. When he was outdoors, all he wanted to do was stand at the fence with his chubby fingers through the links, whining to go outside.

For Alex, the fence was a limit, a restriction— and a highly visible restriction at that. Like many persistent children, Alex sees limits and boundaries in one way only: as something to surmount.

Demanding children who are persistent and insatiable want to experience the world. They don't want to miss anything. Every restriction placed on them feels like a denial, a denial that's keeping them from filling a need.

For some persistent children, like Alex, new experiences are to be found on the other side of the fence, where the grass is definitely greener. For others, however, the experience to be savored is right under her nose. For this child, who has difficulty with transitions, it's very difficult to move from the here and now to a new activity.

"My mother never wanted to take me shopping because she could never move me from one place to another. I would get really interested in one thing, and just *hate* being forced to move on. Once, when I was about five, I got absorbed in watching the produce manager stack grapefruit into a huge pile. I felt that I had to stay and see how high he would be able to stack them. I was so fascinated that I was outraged when my mother pulled me away. I remember digging in my heels and going limp. I also remember being sent to my room when we got home."

Persistent children often have difficulty with transitions, with shifting from one activity to another. That can be evident when it's time to pick up toys and get ready for bed, or when it's time to put away the art supplies and get out the science books at school.

The persistent child usually feels a sense of comfort and control in the activity she's absorbed with at the time. The new activity is less certain, so it's less appealing.

Insatiable children often get stuck in behaviors that aren't really filling any needs. The child who whines relentlessly, for example, is not really happy whining. In those situations, she may need help changing gears and may actually feel better when someone helps her shift to an activity that is more satisfying.

And sometimes demanding and insatiable behaviors intensify when the persistent child is feeling anxious. If she's worried she won't get enough of something, whether it's food, fun, or attention, she may demand more and more. She's asking for reassurance that there will be plenty and that she'll get her fair share.

When the persistent child is thwarted, she often responds with anger. Having something or someone divert her from her goals is intensely frustrating.

WHAT THE DEMANDING CHILD HEARS

Your demanding child's perceptions go beyond what she feels and why she feels it. She also learns to define herself according to what she hears from you and from other people. And because her behavior is often difficult, she receives an excess of negative messages.

She has to cope with being punished for things she may not have intended, or can't control. She has to live with the reactions of teachers who criticize, playmates who hit back, and friends who don't want to be her friend anymore.

At home, she is warned, corrected, ordered about. She hears:

"Can't you stop that jingling sound?"

"All right. Who spilled the juice?"

"Be careful with that!"

"How dare you shout at me!"

The demanding child often hears a whole day-long chorus of "Don'ts." "Don't beat up on your sister." "Don't come in the kitchen with mud on your shoes." "Don't touch the TV remote with peanut butter on your hands." "Don't interrupt."

Then there are the warnings, especially to an impulsive child. "Watch out! Be careful! You'll fall!" Of course, parents issue those warnings in good faith, because they know from experience that their child probably *will* fall or get hurt. But the warnings serve to remind the child of her own shortcomings.

If we're not careful how we talk to our demanding children, our comments to her begin to sound like an endless chorus of "Bad doggie!" It's important to stand back and consider our words, and their effects. We'll discuss this more later on.

THE COMFORT CONNECTION

As parents, we can better understand our demanding children's feelings if we think of their temperament as a comfort zone, a way of behaving that feels most natural to them.

We all seek situations and experiences that are comfortable, and avoid those that are uncomfortable or stressful. And we vary in our perceptions of what's comfortable and what isn't; temperament, to a large degree, determines what behaviors and situations are comfortable.

If we look at our children's temperament from this perspective, it's easier to understand how enduring it is, and how difficult it is for a child to try different ways of behaving.

And yet, challenging children need ways to get along in the world. That means parents need to help children expand the areas in which they feel comfortable, or help them learn how to get along, even if they aren't particularly comfortable.

Since most demanding children are comfortable with action, the key is to help them identify skills and behaviors that will serve them well. They can learn new and better ways to channel their energy, control their impulses, handle their anger, and direct their persistence.

We all have to do things in life that don't come naturally. On any particular morning, we may not feel much like getting out of bed. We may not be inclined to sit through a class that we don't find interesting, or count to ten when someone is provoking us to anger. But as we mature, we accept that these are things that need to be done if we are to live full lives.

As you strive to see the world through your demanding child's eyes, you need to keep in mind this key point: Empathy is essential, but it is not enough. Your child needs to feel your support and understanding, but she also needs to experience the rewards of learning new and better ways to get what she wants out of life.

That means that you need to find and sometimes create opportunities for her to experience growth and success. She'll always have a challenging temperament, but that need not limit her. She will learn new skills and attitudes, and eventually they will become more habitual.

When that happens, the behavior that comes "naturally" to her, and feels comfortable to her, will be more varied and productive.

◆ 5 ◆

Parent Traps: Twenty Well-Meaning Mistakes Parents of Demanding Children Make

Being the parent of a demanding child is difficult, as we detailed in Chapter 3, because so often our children do not respond to the very techniques that work well with most children. If we persist in treating our challenging child the same way we did his older brother or sister, we can stumble into trouble.

Ironically, we stumble precisely because we love our demanding children and want the best for them. We may discipline harshly because we want so badly for them to be well-behaved, or find it impossible to set limits because we want them to be happy. The parents most susceptible to making these errors tend to be the very ones who are most most devoted and conscientious.

Before we examine the specific parental approaches that are most effective in helping challenging children develop and flourish, let's examine some of the common pitfalls that await parents.

The first two points have to do with understanding temperament, and are central to the problem of understanding what makes your child tick. On one hand, parents err by ignoring temperament. On the other, they err by ignoring the child's need for growth.

To illustrate how important both sides of this equation are, let's use the metaphor of a physical condition that can't be cured but needs to be managed.

Suppose your child has poor vision. Suppose you said, "Son, I forbid you to be nearsighted. Please stop this instant."

On the other hand, you might say, "Oh, well, he's a nearsighted kind of guy. What can you do?"

Most likely, you would reject both of those choices. You would have your child's eyes tested and have him fitted with a pair of glasses. You'd teach him how to take care of the glasses and clean the lenses. You might consider getting him contact lenses as he grew older.

You would, in essence, accept him the way he is, and then work to help him thrive despite his shortcomings.

But parents of children with difficult temperaments sometimes fall into the trap of trying to change a child's nature, on one hand, or failing to guide it in positive directions, on the other.

Following are the twenty most common pitfalls:

1. Trying to change basic temperament

"I don't know why you have to fidget like that."

"We'll just have to wait until you're ready to sit still and pay attention."

"She's just doing it to get attention. Ignore her and she'll stop."

"It's no big deal, honey. Don't get so upset over everything."

Statements like these suggest that challenging children can somehow turn into different, more perfect human beings, and do so through an act of will. That's rarely possible. Certainly a demanding child is capable of adapting to parental expectations in many ways, but he is unlikely to be able to change his *essential* temperament. If he is impulsive, he will probably have a lifelong tendency toward impulsivity, although there is much he can do to manage his behavior. He may cope well, even though he may always be quick in his movements and responses.

When parents don't understand temperament and how it guides behavior, they misinterpret their children on several levels. They may not recognize those aspects of behavior that are clearly related to temperament, and they may ascribe negative motives to their child.

In addition, parents who do not understand temperament are less equipped to plan and manage their child's schedule and setting to minimize problems. Telling an impulsive child to "be good" before a visit to a houseful of breakable knickknacks is not the way to help a child succeed.

And it's much harder for parents to monitor the situations that cause difficulties for their children when they aren't aware of what those situations are. They may not pay attention to the cues that indicate their child is losing control and needs redirection. That leaves them surprised and baffled when their child misbehaves.

2. Failure to guide and direct challenging behavior

"Barry knows what he likes. He'll push and push until he gets it. You might as well give him what he wants."

"Jennifer has a short fuse. Better get used to it. That's just the way she is."

Parents like these understand their child's essential nature and have taken a valuable step in helping their demanding child. But they haven't gone far enough. First, they need to stop reinforcing negative behavior. And then work on modifying that behavior.

Demanding children who aren't helped in this way, who remain stuck in behaviors that lead to failure in school or life or leave them isolated or rejected, are being shortchanged.

3. Failure to prioritize

Demanding children often have many traits that cry out for improvement. A child who throws tantrums at home, misbehaves in school, whines, and fights with his friends has so many areas to work on that parents can become obsessed with fixing everything at once.

But there's only so much improving anyone can do at one time, as any adult can attest who has tried to stick to a dozen New Year's resolutions. For a small child, it's going to be next to impossible to succeed at everything.

Parents who try to get a defiant child to behave in school, do his chores without being reminded, sit up straight, stop swearing, play nicely with the neighbor kids, and floss his teeth are setting him and themselves up for failure. The child who is asked to do too much inevitably falls short. He'll be aware that he's falling short, and may lose the will to try.

In addition to singling out the most important areas to work on, it's important not to make too much of trivial aspects of behavior. Your child may have tastes in music or humor that drive you crazy, but those may not be the issues to work on first.

4. Failure to discipline

Setting up appropriate expectations and limits for demanding children is a difficult task. They are, by nature, more rambunctious, impulsive, and stubborn. Rules, it sometimes seems, are meant to be broken, and limits to be stretched.

Because demanding children are difficult to control and difficult to direct, parents sometimes give up the job in despair.

But these children are demanding because they do, in fact, demand more from parents. And discipline is one of their fundamental needs. They need limits, whether they like them or not, and their behavior will not improve if they aren't given loving guidance.

5. Using negative language

Language is an essential part of any child's self-image and sense of worth. Children learn to think highly of themselves from the favorable words they hear from people they love. The demanding child, however, is at particular risk for negative messages, because so much of his behavior is unacceptable, or invites correction from a whole range of people as he goes through his day:

"Can't you sit still?"

"He's such a brat."

"Will you stop bugging me?"

"Don't let him play. He'll just wreck everything."

Negative language that labels a child has three effects:

• It demeans him. Words like "terror" and "troublemaker" may seem accurate to an outside observer. But demanding children are not helped by hearing those labels.

• It deprives him of a sense that his feelings and inclinations are real and valid, and that the way he is and the way he sees the world has validity. Saying, "Now, don't get mad" when he *is* getting mad creates the sense that he shouldn't feel what he's feeling.

• It gives him a sense of powerlessness. "I'm hopeless. No matter what I do, I just get in trouble. Why even try?"

Parents of challenging children often find themselves asking lots of "Why" questions of their children, such as: "Why did you run out into the street? Don't you realize you could get hit by a car?" or "Why did you hit Rasheed?" or "Why do you keep asking me that over and over again?"

These are rhetorical questions that really don't have an acceptable answer. Usually, the child doesn't know.

Sarcasm is another way in which exasperated parents use language in unconstructive ways.

"Oh, great. Why don't you just break the *rest* of them, too?"

"Throwing sand is a really good way of getting your friends to let you play."

"Thank you for interrupting me while I'm on the phone."

Sarcasm is hostile language. And it is hard for children to sort out the distinction between the stated words and the implied ones, especially when they're quite young. Surely you aren't thanking your child for interrupting you? Are you supposed to throw sand?

Unfortunately, adults do sometimes revert to sarcasm when they are annoyed and irritated—and demanding children can certainly annoy and irritate us. But remember that sarcasm is a form of thinly repressed anger.

In Chapter 6, we'll discuss ways to describe the demanding child's behavior objectively, but in a way that respects the child and leads to better behavior.

6. Yelling

Shouting and yelling as a means of guiding our children is generally not effective. They may be stubborn, balky, resistant to following orders, or out of control, but sometimes the behavior is not under their control. And children who are already easily angered are rarely improved by being screamed at.

But most of all, angry words or an angry tone of voice from a parent can feel like a personal rejection to a child—even a tough, feisty, demanding child.

When yelling becomes a habit, however, it can be easily tuned out by demanding kids. When that happens, it undermines the parent's sense of competence and effectiveness. There's nothing more deflating than shouting orders at someone who doesn't respond at all.

7. Praising out-of-control behavior

"Boy, he doesn't hold anything back!" says the proud father as his angry son shrieks with rage in a public playground.

"You sure know what you want, don't you," says the mother of a child who is nagging relentlessly for a particular candy bar.

It's fine to honor your child's unique personality, but praising, or seeming to praise, a negative element of his behavior will reinforce it and make it harder to change. It would be better for the noisy child in the playground to hear something like, "We know you feel strongly, Alex, but you need to use words, not screams."

8. Vagueness and inconsistency

Your demanding child needs to know where he stands. If you say, "Now, behave when we go into Aunt Rachel's house," you're probably not giving him enough information. Whatever his style of demanding behavior, he'll do better if he knows exactly what you mean: "Remember the rule about visiting. You'll need to stay near me. If you want to touch Aunt Rachel's paperweight collection, you'll need to ask her for permission. And remember to say 'Thank you' when she gives you a drink."

If your child is persistent, vague suggestions or half-hearted requests will fall on deaf ears. Similarly, if you are inconsistent—enforcing a rule one day, letting it pass the next—your persistent child will become less likely to comply.

Four-year-old Ben is climbing on the stair bannister again, against the rules. His mother, who is talking on the phone, says, sternly, "Ben, get down from there. You might fall and hurt yourself." Ben gets down, but lingers near the scene of the crime. His mother returns her attention to her telephone conversation and becomes so absorbed that when Ben climbs on the bannister again, he isn't stopped.

As we've said, the rules and suggestions that apply to most children are often less effective with demanding children. For example, flexibility can be a virtue. Easing up on the rules from time to time and letting the child win a few battles can be a healthy and positive way of relieving tension when the child is fairly easygoing and cooperative anyway. But flexibility and an "Oh, all right, just this once" approach can be just the wrong message for a child whose normal style is to fight and resist your demands.

9. Inconsistency between parents

Demanding children need two main things that are, on the surface, contradictory: They need loving acceptance and approval, on one hand, and they need limits and firmness on the other. Sometimes parents each take a piece of that whole: Dad, for example, may be the kindly, accepting, indulgent parent, while Mom takes on the role of the "heavy."

And each parent is right—but only half right.

When parents split these functions and assign one wholly to one parent and the other wholly to the other, their lack of a united front makes it harder for the child to modify his behavior. Of course, parents naturally differ in their own temperaments and their own way of relating to a child, but they're more effective when they can pull in the same direction on behalf of their demanding child.

10. Counting on consequences

When parents rely too much on natural or logical consequences to help a demanding child improve behavior, they're failing to consider the particular needs of temperament.

Less challenging children often do well under a system that rewards or punishes through natural outcomes of actions. If a child goes outside without a jacket, the natural outcome is that she feels cold. Eventually, she'll think to wear the jacket. Similarly, a logical consequence might be that if she is careless with her library books and loses them, she has to pay for them with her own money.

The idea behind these consequences is that they are effective because they grow directly out of the child's action, and are not imposed arbitrarily. A spanking, for example, is not a logical consequence of losing library books.

But demanding children often don't see the logic, or don't seem to mind the consequences. They may continue the action even though the "outcome" is undesirable. Persistent children, in particular, have trouble stopping undesirable behavior. And impulsive children often aren't able to think ahead well enough to avoid the "natural punishment" of consequences.

Matt, for example, is an energetic, impulsive child who spills frequently. When Matt's in the kitchen, it's guaranteed that something will end up all over the floor. Matt's parents move carefully and watch what they're doing, because they want to avoid the hassle of cleaning up big spills.

But Matt doesn't *mind* wiping up spills. For him, that's all part of the game. And that means that the consequences that motivate his parents don't motivate him.

11. Assigning motives

Demanding children can be stubborn and exasperating. It's easy for parents to fall into the trap of assigning motives to their children that aren't necessarily present. This is particularly true when parent and child have different temperaments. The parent is mystified by what motivates the child and says, "He's doing this just to drive me crazy!"

It's easy to miscalculate when trying to guess a child's motives. Most children aren't being the way they are in order to make us have a bad day. They're acting that way because it's their nature, or because they don't know how to behave better. Impugning their motives makes them feel wronged and misunderstood.

Assigning motives also contributes to a victim mentality in parents and puts the child in the driver's seat, rather than helping the parents muster the authority and confidence they need.

12. Failure to take care of parental needs

Parents of demanding children are under considerable stress, as we outlined in Chapter 3. Yet they're at risk of becoming so tied up in their child's needs that they ignore their own. A parent whose needs aren't met will be less able to nurture a demanding child.

When the flight attendant on an airliner explains the function of the emergency oxygen mask, she always reminds passengers traveling with young children to remember to put their own mask on first, then assist the children. The reason is obvious—an adult who faints from oxygen deprivation isn't much use to a child. But it's just as plain why the reminder is necessary: we have a natural impulse to assist a child, to cater to the needs of a child. But fulfilling a child's needs at the expense of our own ultimately does a disservice to both.

13. Overanalyzing

It's important to understand our children and what makes them tick. It's important to understand temperament, and what lies behind their actions. But sometimes we're afraid to do anything until we're convinced we understand what lies behind our child's behavior, with the result that we take *no* action. "Are you angry at Mommy because she went to work?" Or, "I wonder why Elena is so demanding of attention? Is it because of the new baby?"

Asking those questions is fine, but there comes a point when you need to act on the information you have. At some point, it's time to focus on the behavior itself.

14. Reflecting your child's negatives

If your child is angry, it's easy to become angry yourself, even if that's not your usual way of behaving. If your child is locked in and resisting something past the point of common sense, it's easy to get locked into your own resistance.

Demanding children have a way of bringing out the worst in us. When this happens, it's important to recognize the situation and step back into your adult role with a comment like, "Laurie, I can see that we're both stuck here. This discussion isn't going anywhere for either of us. Let's come back to it after dinner."

15. Allowing parents' early experiences to define expectations

"I remember enjoying Barbie dolls so much when I was Nicole's age. My best friend and I would spend hours in her room acting out all sorts of fantasies. But Nicole just ignores her dolls. She hates doing anything quiet in her room. She'd rather be on the go, going to soccer practice or dance class. That's fine, but I don't want her to miss the fun I remember."

"I remember how miserable I was at camp when I hadn't remembered to pack comfortable socks and sunburn lotion. I got badly burned, and could hardly walk from all my blisters. My son gets furious when I insist that he pack the right things and promise me he'll use them. He says it doesn't matter, that he'll be fine, but I worry he'll suffer the way I did."

"I was such a troublemaker in school. I straightened out in high school, but I was behind academically. Now I see some of that same behavior in my third-grader."

In many ways, parents try to provide their children with what they themselves missed. If they grew up poor or didn't get an education, they struggle to give their children better opportunities. Parents do this with emotional experiences as well, trying to protect their children from remembered hurts and supplying them with remembered pleasures.

However, we are not our children. We can't undo our own childhood disappointments through them, nor can we relive our childhood pleasures in the same way. Our children will experience their own challenges and delights, not ours.

16. Overprotecting

Ironically, parents who *do* understand and recognize their child's temperament can be at risk of doing too much to protect him from the consequences of his behavior.

They may bail him out of the trouble he gets himself into, breaking up backyard disputes to keep him from losing his temper, making apologies for him, preparing his breakfast because otherwise he's certain to cut himself or break the dishes.

If he complains that his soccer teammates aren't being fair, his parents may pull him off the team, "protecting" him from an experience that might teach him valuable lessons in cooperation. Or parents might try to hide a child's failings by being evasive during conferences with his teacher.

It's less trouble, in the short run, to overprotect than it is to hold our demanding child responsible for his behavior. However, it hinders his development in three ways:

• Overprotection reinforces the child's temperamental bias and does not allow him to develop the skills he needs.

• It sends a negative message. It says, "You can't take care of yourself. I have to do it for you."

• Overprotective parents can get so caught up in their child's needs and all the subtle dimensions of his temperament that they genuinely come to believe that nobody else can possibly understand him. Who else could meet his needs, keep him functioning? It's easy to start doing too much for a child, instead of helping him do more for himself.

17. Comparing

"Why can't you sit still like Erica?"

"I was responsible when I was your age. In fact, I was already allowed to cut the grass with a power mower."

"Those children over there are playing nicely and quietly. Can't you boys do the same?"

Comparing your child to other children makes him feel like a failure. It makes him feel unappreciated and rejected. Rather than motivating them to do better, it makes him feel resentful and jealous.

Sometimes parents compare their demanding children not to his peers, but with the way they were as a child (or the way they *think* they were).

"I was careful with my things. I didn't fiddle with the stapler until I broke it. I didn't break every glass in the house."

It's one thing to offer encouragement with stories about your childhood, or to share with your child how you solved a problem when you were his age. It's another to belabor the issue about how much better you were than your demanding child is now.

18. Assuming that they're tough because they act tough

A child who is strong, defiant, and determined can present quite a forceful presence. And sometimes demanding children have a knack for acting as if they know the score, aren't concerned about punishment, don't care what anyone thinks.

But generally, they do care, and are concerned. They need as much tenderness and understanding as any small child who is still in the process of growing capable and confident.

Demanding children often have problems with self-esteem and self-confidence. Just because they walk with a swagger doesn't mean they don't need to be nurtured and supported.

19. Forgetting that they'll grow up

Demanding children often behave in ways that, understandably, worry parents. If your child has explosive tantrums at age five, it's natural to think, "What if he has these same tantrums when he's ten or twelve?" When we extrapolate what we see today into the future, we're forgetting that in five years your child will have five additional years of maturation and learning. It's better to keep a positive attitude and focus on the present.

However, it's important not to get stuck with expectations that your demanding child may have already grown beyond. If you set priorities and your child has made improvement in the important areas, don't forget to review his progress and see if he's ready to take on more challenges. As he grows, you'll "raise the bar" of your expecations.

Maybe when your child was four, you were ecstatic if he got through a playdate without biting anyone. Now that he's eight, the standards for success can be higher.

20. Perfectionism

If your child is demanding, he will always be challenging to some degree. There is no way to convert him into an entirely different child. Your life together may always involve some compromises, some give-and-take.

And if your child isn't perfect, neither are you. You will probably never get the Perfect Parent of the Year award. You will do better at some aspects of your parenting job, and less well at others. Dwelling only on the failures blinds you to all the successes, big and small, that you and your child have achieved.

You can't do anything about your child's genetic blueprint, or his prenatal environment, or whether his temperament harmonizes with your own. However, as we outlined in Chapter 1, the way you accept, manage, and direct your child's temperament—the interaction between his innate personality and life experience—is what sets your child's course for the future.

Many of the mistakes parents make with their demanding children are the natural outgrowth of their desire to help and encourage.

Often a head-on approach to solving temperament problems isn't the best way. The most effective approach is often indirect, and almost counterintuitive, the way you see a faint star more clearly by looking at it indirectly.

In the following chapter, we'll outline techniques for working with—not against—your child's challenging temperament and helping him grow.

◆ 6 ◆

Techniques That Work: What Really Helps Your Demanding Child Thrive and Grow

When Derek's family sits down to watch a video together, everyone sprawls on the couch and collects the necessary props: television remote, snacks, and Lego set. The Legos are for Derek. He's so energetic and fidgety that unless he has something in his hands, he'll pick at the seams of the upholstery or reach for the wallpaper and peel it off—all without realizing what his fingers are doing. He knows that the house rule is: No sitting on the couch unless you have something to fiddle with.

Before going to bed at night, Melissa counts up her small hoard of blue poker chips. One more day has gone by and Melissa hasn't spilled once, earning a token for each disaster-free meal and snack.

Carlos has just come home from school, without his math book. His mother says he'll have to call a classmate and arrange to borrow the book so he can do his homework. Carlos had wanted to play, and he's furious. His voice gets more angry, his mother's voice gets more angry. Then Carlos stands up and says in a tight voice, "I'm getting upset. I need to be alone for a few minutes." With that, he stalks from the room to cool off.

These are all demanding children, yet they're all busy growing and thriving with their demanding temperaments. They're learning to live with energy, control impulsivity, manage anger and moderate persistence in an acceptable way. Of course, they're still kids, so they have a long way to go. But with their parents' support, they're making great strides.

As we said in the previous chapters, your demanding child needs, more than anything, to be loved and cherished for the unique person she is.

Your child also needs, more than anything, your help in managing and directing her demanding behavior. She needs to acquire skills and experiences that will help her flourish, even if acquiring those skills and experiences does not come naturally to her.

If a difficult child is indulged but not guided, the results are disastrous for the family that lives with her, the school that tries to educate her, and the community where she lives. But it's also unfortunate for the child herself, whose opportunities for success and acceptance are curtailed.

But if the emphasis is on correction only, her spirit will be broken, or she will expend her considerable energies fighting you and fighting authority, instead of channeling it into productive and satisfying activities.

Demanding children need both sides of this equation. Following are some techniques that help them meet those needs in general terms. Later on, we'll discuss specific suggestions for specific traits.

Teach her about temperament

Even very little children can learn about temperament and the ways that people differ in how they approach the world.

You're teaching her whenever you say to your high-energy child, "You're the kind of girl who likes to be busy. Some people like to move around a lot."

As your child grows, you can explain what you've learned about the biological basis for certain aspects of behavior. You can remind your child that being particularly energetic, intense, persistent, or quick-on-the-uptake are all valuable traits that have helped individuals and groups survive.

As you teach your demanding child about her temperament, be sure to teach her about yours, too. If yours is different from hers, you'll need to explain about fit and why some things she does are difficult for you to tolerate not because of her but because of you.

Whether your own temperament is similar to your child's or quite different, you can discuss it with her. You might say, "I know you like to have someone to talk to when you come home, and you get restless if you have to be by yourself. I'm the kind of person who finds it restful to be alone some of the time. That's one of the ways we're different."

Your child will need to learn how to relate to lots

of people, some of them sensitive or easily irritated or shy. You do your child a favor when you teach her to understand other people and their differences.

Watch your language

How you talk to your child about her temperament, and the words she acquires to describe herself, are essential both to her self-esteem and to her ability to regulate her behavior.

From her earliest years, she'll benefit from knowing and using the right terms for feelings, actions, and tendencies. If your two-year-old dashes around the playground like a tornado, or your four-year-old resists your request that she stop what she's doing and get ready for bed, you can use words like "energy" and "bouncy" and "determined."

The key to defining your child's temperament in an affirming, positive way, is to use positive words for the most basic, unchanging aspects of temperament. Those are qualities that make her herself, that make her special. You might say, "Everyone else got all tired out at the skating rink, but you kept going and going! You've got what it takes to be a champ!"

You needn't sugar-coat a particular behavior that your child needs to change. But you can define how she *feels* in positive ways.

For example:

• Instead of "You're too fidgety!" you can say, "Your fingers need to be busy."

• Instead of saying, "You've got a terrible temper," you can say, "You have intense feelings. Your whole body shows how strongly you feel." Or, "You care very deeply about things being fair."

• Instead of, "You're stubborn," you can say, "You're persistent," or, "When you know what you want, you're very determined."

You'll notice that the negative phrases bring the discussion to a halt. All they do is label and express disapproval.

But the positive phrases open the door to constructive suggestions and helpful discussions, like "What would those busy fingers like to play with while we're on the airplane?" Or, "Can you think of something you can do with those strong feelings? Is there a way to solve this that's fair?"

Remember that demanding children receive more than their share of negative words and descriptions as they go through their day. Other adults and children call attention to their excesses and label them in ways that aren't always thoughtful or pleasant. Make your child's home the place where the people who love her will do their best to put a positive spin on her birthright.

Give her time

Be realistic about progress. Demanding children take time to grow, and they take time to improve their behavior. Present new demands and experiences gradually, and according to your child's individual rate of development.

But demanding children do grow up, and the tasks she couldn't manage last year may be manageable this year.

Prioritize

Setting priorities is essential with demanding children because they have to work harder at developmental tasks. They can't afford to have their focus deflected by minor issues.

There are some issues of discipline, schedule, safety, and courtesy that are non-negotiable. Your child has to go to school, may not play in the street, and must not hurt the baby.

Other issues just are less important. Your task is to reduce battles over trivial items and save your heavy fire for the things that really matter.

The Essentials

The safety of your child, and of other people, is one of the essentials. Your demanding child must learn to adhere to age-appropriate safety rules, or be closely supervised until she can. She must not be permitted to hurt other children or put them at risk.

For some demanding children who express anger physically, for example, learning to stop biting or hitting is an essential, a first order of priority.

Education is another essential. Whether or not your child likes going to school or likes the teacher, she does need to become educated. The details of which school, program, or teacher may be subject to negotiation or compromise.

Rudiments of courtesy are essentials, because without them, she will not be able to earn the acceptance and social approval she needs.

These are the must-dos, and you and your child should concentrate on these.

The Nonessentials

This list will depend in part on what your own personal tastes and limits are. But in general, assuming your demanding child is focusing on the essentials, it's probably not absolutely essential that her clothes match, that she make her bed, or that she sit quietly through a long concert or lecture if she's an active child.

If your child uses slang that you find silly and unappealing, or if she has a habit of fidgeting with her hair, those issues may not be worth the aggravation of addressing while you've got more important things to do.

The Negotiables

Then there are the items that fall in between. This is the realm of deal-making and compromise. Behaviors like complaining, sulking, poor table manners, or making rude noises for comic effect may be in this category. These are issues that might be worth working on if they bother you, but could be delayed until more serious matters have been attended to. The key is to concentrate on a few essential behaviors first.

Sometimes the act of setting priorities and letting

go of some of the less important items can be a great relief to parent and child alike. "Once I decided I wasn't going to focus on Jared's messy room," said one mother, "I felt liberated. I'd been nagging him about that room because I felt it was my sacred mission to make him responsible and perfect. But it generated endless stress for both of us, and I had less energy to get him to focus on the important tasks: managing his temper, and doing his share of other household responsibilities."

Jared's mother isn't going to ignore issues of tidiness and personal responsibility as Jared grows older. It's just that she's moved them to the back burner for the time being.

Emphasize progress

Take every opportunity to point out to your demanding child the progress she's made. "You waited until I got off the phone before you asked your question. I know that's not easy for you, but you did it. I appreciate that."

Praise the small step she just made. Don't immediately turn to the giant leap she still has to accomplish. If you do, you seem impossible to satisfy and she'll be less enthusiastic about trying.

When your first-grader comes home beaming and shouts, "Mom! I got a star for courtesy!" you would praise her accomplishment on its own merits. A less appropriate response would be to say, "Great! How many more stars do you need to get Best of the Month?"

Even as you praise the baby steps your child takes, take care not to gush. Excess or insincere praise suggests that you don't have confidence in her ability to do the job. Your challenging child needs to feel capable of managing her difficult behavior, and she'll do better in an atmosphere of calm enthusiasm.

A final note about praising: Don't put it off! You may have heard the phrase, "Catch your child being good." It means that you should pay attention to your child when she's behaving well, not just when she needs correction. It's constructive advice for parents of demanding children, too—*but you have to be fast!* With impulsive children, in particular, your window of opportunity may be quite small. Your child may be setting the table with great care, setting each glass down carefully. In the blink of an eye, however, she may have rushed to answer the phone, knocked over the trash can and stepped in the dog's water dish. So praise and reinforce right away, while you can.

Focus on behavior, not emotions

When you correct your child, try to focus on her actions, not the feelings that provoked it. Your child has a right to feel what she feels, but she is responsible for what she chooses to do about those feelings. She may feel angry or impatient or disgruntled, but she doesn't have to lash out or have a tantrum.

Give a demonstration

Don't limit your help to words alone. Instead of just telling your child what to do and not to do, show her how. This is especially useful when she needs to learn better ways to perform a physical act.

You might show her how to hug her friends more gently so they don't feel assaulted. You can demonstrate how to close the shower door gently, or put the juice pitcher back into the refrigerator without knocking over everything on the shelf. You can demonstrate how she can take a deep breath when she's angry and how to ask for attention in a courteous way.

Remind her that things get easier

If you've ever applied for a mortgage, started a new job, changed a tire, or prepared your own taxes, you know that tasks that seem overwhelming the first time you do them seem easier the second and third times.

If your demanding child is old enough to understand, convey to her that adults, too, have to learn to control their impulses and follow rules and get along with others.

As your child progresses, your reminders can include references to her own accomplishments. "Remember how I had to hold your hand when we came to this museum last time? You really liked to grab everything you saw. You're older now, and you know how to behave in a museum all by yourself.''

Hold a dress rehearsal

Role playing and rehearsing are effective tools for building skills. If your child has trouble controlling her anger, you can practice conflict resolution techniques with role playing. If she is relentless in her demands for attention, you can practice ways for her to ask for things in an appropriate way.

For example, you might play the role of the teacher or adult friend who is busy and ignores her requests for a moment. She can practice being patient and asking for what she wants in a polite voice.

You can also change roles to give your demanding child a chance to get a better sense of how her behavior affects others. If she pushes other children out of the way or grabs toys from their hands, you can show her how those actions feel, and how different the gentler actions feel to the person on the receiving end.

If your preschooler has trouble with transitions, you can make a teddy bear or puppet take on her role. "Teddy has trouble getting ready for bed. Let's see if we can teach him what he does first. When he's all ready, how many stories will we read him?" The key is to put your child into the role of teacher or mentor, so that she gets experience helping a persistent teddy bear get through a difficult time of day.

Keep on hugging

As your demanding child grows, make an effort to keep physical affection in your relationship. Naturally the form this takes will change as your cuddly toddler becomes a gangly preteen. But when you give and receive a hug, ruffle your child's hair or offer a friendly pat on the back, that physical affection communicates your love and caring eloquently, especially at times when everyone's been tense and not communicating positively with words.

Keep a sense of humor

Humor is a great way to relieve tension and keep things in perspective. Be capable of laughing at an absurd situation, and laugh at your own foibles and mistakes.

Humor, also, is a great way to encourage a balky child's cooperation. If you've asked your daughter several times to feed the dog, and she remains glued to the television, you might be tempted to issue a punishment. Instead, consider acting silly: Get down on all fours, barking and whining like a hungry dog until she takes action.

Humor and silliness can defuse situations because they allow a stubborn child to cooperate without losing face.

But don't make the error of laughing *at* your child or trivializing her difficulties. Laughter and humor are positive when all parties find them enjoyable.

When children are defiant and angry, also, it's important to take their anger seriously. No one likes to be told, "You're so cute when you're mad," when they really are upset about an injustice. That includes children, too.

Honor the total child, not just the temperament

Give your demanding child other ways to define herself than just temperament labels. Even the positive ones we've described don't encompass the complexity of the whole child. Your impulsive daughter might be a talented pianist; your persistent son might have a knack for getting the dog to behave. Whatever other positive traits your child has should be stressed. Temperament is important, but don't let it limit how you define your child.

Following are some techniques for helping your child manage according to her fundamental style.

THE HIGH-ENERGY CHILD

• Provide plenty of opportunity for active play. Do not expect your child to be still for long periods of time. If you know she'll be expected to be controlled for an extended period, like at school, before traveling or before church, give her a chance to do what's comfortable—which means move around.

• Some energetic children gain energy from vigorous activity, instead of dissipating it. If that's the case, try limiting the length of physical activities. Change the game, change the scene, make her change gears and downshift her energy.

• Provide cooling-off periods. A child who tends to get wild and out of control may need to give herself a time-out to cool down.

• Use rewards as transitions. "After tennis, we'll stop and rent a movie."

• Intervene early if she appears to be growing tense and fidgety. If you're traveling in the car, and she's getting antsy in the back seat, try to stop for a break *before* she gets out of control.

• High-energy children often come off as aggressive when they're really just strong. Alex, a strong, energetic three-year-old, likes to hug people when he meets them. Trouble is, he just about squashes them when he does this, and he often knocks other kids over. But he's really not being aggressive or hostile. Alex needs to learn how to hug carefully.

• High-energy children are often very loud. If your child is clearly bothering others with her voice, you can teach her to monitor. Show her how other people look when they are uncomfortable with noise—they put their hands over their ears, or they turn away. Show her how they'll be more accepting when she tones down the noise level.

Sing with your child, encouraging her to use all kinds of vocal tones in her singing from loud bellowing to soft whispers. You can do the same with story telling, too. She might take the part of the noisy giant some of the time, and the meek little mouse other times.

Teach your child the difference between an "inside" voice and an "outside" voice. Screeching and bellowing belong outside or in informal settings; try not to reward an inappropriate voice with your attention.

And when your child does control her volume appropriately, be sure to praise her pleasant voice.

THE IMPULSIVE CHILD

• Chart your child's negative behavior. Is there a pattern to it? Does she show less control when she is tired, hungry, or distracted? Is there a particular setting in which it's hard for her to stay calm?

• Involve your child in activities that reinforce cause-and-effect lessons and natural consequences. Hands-on activities like cooking, for example, are rich in lessons, and the results are immediately apparent: If you add the water too fast, it splashes out of the bowl. But if you carry the eggs carefully, they don't break.

• When you read stories with your child, pause and ask her to think of what happens next, or what the character will do in a situation.

• Play "What If?" with your child. Practice thinking out outcomes and consequences. "What will happen if we don't put gas in the car before we drive to Grandpa's?"

• Reward patience and planning behavior when your child demonstrates it.

• Recognize and accept that your impulsive child may require closer supervision than her less-impulsive friends, and may require it longer. Base your decisions about what your child can handle on her proven capabilities, rather than her age: Your child can be trusted to stay at home by herself when you believe she's ready, not necessarily when her friends are allowed to be alone.

• Have faith that impulsivity does moderate with maturity. All young children, whether they're demanding or not, have elements of this trait. Your impulsive child will improve with time and experience.

THE ANGRY CHILD

• Teach your angry child what anger is, what it feels like, and what its uses are. Her intense feelings can motivate her to fix what's bothering her, but they can also get her in trouble.

• Encourage your child to express anger with words ("That's not fair!") instead of with actions.

• Teach anger-managing techniques. She can count to ten before exploding, which often prevents an explosion. She can take three big breaths. She can ask for help with a frustrating tasks. If she is angry at you, she can say why in words, not screams.

• Help your child distinguish between healthy and unhealthy anger. If your child is angry because she was bullied on the playground, that's healthy anger. If she loses control and spends the rest of recess kicking all the other kids, that's not healthy anger.

• Teach etiquette. Of course, good manners are important for any child to learn. But for angry children, there's great value in the ritual habits of courtesy. Saying "please," "thank you," and "excuse me" are time-honored tricks for managing minor disputes and keeping them from becoming major.

• Acknowledge your child's anger when she expresses it. One thing anger does that can be constructive is to let others know we mean business—that this is SERIOUS! Attention must be paid! So when your child explodes with anger, you may dislike the display and you may be embarrassed and upset about the situation, but you do need to let her know that she has gotten her message across. "I can see that you're angry, Katie. When you're able to talk about it, I'm ready to listen."

• She can release the powerful tensions of anger in appropriate ways. She might take a bike ride, or punch a pillow, or write her feelings in a letter. As she grows older, she may benefit from relaxation and visualization techniques to regain her calm.

• Know what triggers tantrums and outbursts in your child. If she typically loses control when she's frustrated with an inanimate object (like a bottle that won't open or a vending machine that won't yield a drink), be ready to help before she loses control.

• For young children in particular, self-talk is helpful in internalizing messages. You can demonstrate self-talk yourself, by saying, "I'm mad at Mrs. Smith, but I'm not going to yell. I'm going to keep cool." Soon, your child can say things like, "Hitting hurts. I better not."

• Sometimes angry children seem bent on provoking their own anger. In that case, try to avoid being drawn into it.

Nine-year-old Kevin knew that he wasn't going to be allowed to invite friends to sleep over until a major redecorating project was complete. Every room in the house was being painted, and the furniture would be covered or out of place until the work was completed.

Kevin came home from school and first nagged about the inadequacy of the snack supply. He carped about everything, finding small ways to build up his resentment. Finally he said, "I haven't had a sleepover in weeks. Can I have a sleepover tonight?"

Kevin knew, when he asked, that the answer would be no. He asked the question for the express purpose of getting a nice, ripe excuse for an outburst.

Kevin's mother was tempted to scream and rave, "Of course not! You know you can't, so why did you even ask?" Instead, she said, "Kevin, we've talked about all this. What do you think?" Kevin still fussed, but at least the answer came from him, not his mother.

Sometimes anger becomes chronic and debilitating, or explodes into aggressive and destructive behavior. We discuss these dimensions of anger in Chapter 7.

THE PERSISTENT CHILD

• Give your persistent, insatiable child choices. When she fulfills her needs through her own actions, that helps her feel satisfied. People who feel powerless try to get their needs met through begging or whining. Confident people act or negotiate.

When your child makes good choices, praise her judgment. You might say, "You're a good shopper. Those grapes you picked out were sure sweet."

Be careful not to praise in a way that seems to preempt her choice, in effect saying, "Good! You picked the one I wanted you to!"

• Don't negotiate with a gun to your head. Negotiations with persistent children can feed the frenzy of whining and nagging. If you feel you're being pressured or worn down, bring the discussion to a halt. Say, "You've told me what you want. I need to think about it. We'll talk again later."

• Be clear and explicit about rules, expectations, and limits: One hour at the playground, and not longer. Two cookies each. Period. Persistent, insistent children look at vagueness as a sign of weakness and a signal to begin testing.

• Persistent chidren who tend to be intrusive need clear rules about physical and personal boundaries. Your child needs to accept that you and others need privacy. She needs to learn to knock on doors before opening them. She needs to stay at her own table in restaurants.

• Give your child the chance to practice establishing her own limits. Often, we impose so much structure that insatiable children keep up their habits because they never get the chance to try to stop themselves. At some point, she needs practice trying to set limits on her own and learn what it feels like to stop herself.

• Encourage your child to limit complaining behavior. As she gets a bit older, you can tell her that complaining a lot tends to make other people pull away from her, so she'll need to learn how to control it.

• Take advantage of the strengths that this trait brings with it. Your persistent child will be a real champion at following routines.

• Whining is an occupational hazard of persistent children who get stuck in negative behaviors. If you reward whines with attention and acquiescence, you'll reinforce the behavior. If you try to ignore a whine and hope it will stop on its own, chances are you'll run out of patience before your child runs out of whines.

The first step is to make sure your child understands what a whine is, how it differs from an acceptable tone of voice, and what its effect on other people is. Next, announce that requests need to be made in a regular tone of voice, not a whine.

If your persistent child asks for attention with a whine, say, "I hear a whine. If you ask in a regular voice, I'll listen to you."

COPING WITH TRANSITIONS

Changing gears from one activity to another is particularly difficult for children who are insatiable and persistent. And that can make getting through the day hard on everyone. Just getting your child out of bed, dressed, fed, to school, in from play, through the homework hour, and back to bed can feel like running a marathon. Here are some techniques:

• Give your persistent child advance warning before any change. Instead of making her do something right that minute, give her just a bit of slack:

"In five minutes, it will be time to get out of the pool."

"At the next commercial, please bring down your clothes hamper."

"Three more swings, then jump off and we'll get in the car."

• Set a timer and place it near your child as she is winding down an activity. That way she begins the process of reminding herself of an upcoming change of scene. You could also use a windup toy, a music box, or a short piece of taped music.

• For an older child especially, encourage input into deciding when to stop what she's doing. She might want to finish her picture before she has to clean up her paints. Or she may have one page left of a chapter. She'll be more able to make a change when you let her have some say. Once she's picked one, however, do hold her to it.

• Budget more time for transitions and warnings than you need with your other children.

• Use imagination and humor to ease transitions. The horsey ride up the stairs to bed is a time-honored way to make transitions more palatable. So is putting the toy animals to bed before taking a nap, or buckling up into the space-ship (car seat) and blasting off on Saturday morning errands. When you keep the fun in daily activities, it makes it easier for persistent children to change gears.

THE DEMANDING CHILD AND DISCIPLINE

Your challenging child needs limits and discipline like any other child. As we outlined in Chapter 5, parents of demanding children sometimes find it difficult to set effective limits. But a demanding child will not be able to improve her behavior without structure and guidance.

Discipline does not need to be harsh in order to be effective. In fact, the less you actually punish, the more effective you will be as a parent.

Psychologist Diana Baumrind has outlined three basic parental styles of limit setting: the *authoritarian*, the *permissive*, and the *authoritative* styles.

The authoritarian parent relies on strict rules and harsh discipline. Children in an authoritarian family may appear obedient, but they obey out of fear rather than from internalizing the reasons for good behavior. And demanding children may become more defiant under authoritarian rule.

The permissive parent emphasizes rapport and understanding, and relies on the child's inner virtues to guide him. Punishment is almost nonexistent. Children of permissive parents may do well if they are naturally compliant and cooperative, but demanding children often fail to develop any control of their behavior.

The authoritative parent strikes a balance between these extremes. This parent maintains rapport and communicates the rules and the reasons behind them. But rules are backed up with structure and consequences, although actual punishment is kept to a minimum.

The authoritative style is probably best for all children, but for demanding children it's the only sensible approach.

Within this style, it's important to work with your knowledge of your child's particular demanding trait. Otherwise, you'll apply approaches that might work with other children but not your own.

For example, most children very much want to please their parents. But an angry child, at least during her most intense moods, wants to lash out, not please.

Most children can rein in their behavior by thinking about the consequences of their actions. But impulsive children don't plan their actions much, so they're not as likely choose wisely.

Persistent children have difficulty stopping inappropriate behavior once it has begun. Ignoring their negative behavior and hoping it will go away on its own is not generally effective.

FOUR TECHNIQUES FOR EFFECTIVE DISCIPLINE

• **Depersonalize limits.** Demanding children resist limits naturally, and may seem to take them as a personal affront. Whenever possible, de-emphasize the power struggle, and stress the immutable, natural law aspects of limits: "Yes, it's clear that you're having a good time playing video games, but the rule is nine o'clock bedtime on school nights."

• **Focus on the behavior, not the temperament.** Naturally you will take into account your child's demanding traits as you establish expectations and consequences. But when you reprimand or correct your child, you'll say something like, "I know you feel angry at Mark, but hitting is not allowed. You'll have time-out for hitting."

• **"Enhance" the natural and logical consequences of misbehavior.** As we've said, demanding children often don't seem as receptive to these natural outcomes as more easygoing children. Like Matt, who didn't mind spilling because he didn't mind the extra work involved in cleaning up, you may have to reinforce consequences. Matt might be more careful if he knew he'd have to pay for the soda or juice he wasted. Or he might respond better to a star chart that rewarded him for being careful.

• **Avoid physical punishment.** Harsh punishment is the least effective way to guide behavior in demanding children. The most effective punishments are consistent and short. If you issue a timeout when your four-year-old breaks a house rule about snacks in the living room, a few minutes should be as effective as a half hour. For older children, the most effective technique is withholding privileges—and the expectation that the child will make amends to earn the privileges back.

CHARTING BETTER BEHAVIOR

A reward chart is one of the most effective methods for tracking your child's progress once you've identified a few specific areas that need improvement and your child has agreed to make the effort. Teachers make effective use of charts and systems of tangible rewards and prizes from gold stars to stickers to pencils.

Whether it's pinned to the bulletin board in your child's room, or attached to the refrigerator with magnets, a behavior and reward chart can be effective because it makes progress and goals concrete, and allows your child to focus her energies on a few important tasks. And she can see at a glance how she is progressing toward a reward.

To be effective, the chart needs to be simple and focus on only a few behaviors. Those behaviors need to be actions your child can reasonably be expected to control and that are appropriate to her age. A young, impulsive child might earn stars for getting through a day without spilling. An older, angry child might earn points for speaking courteously to family members. A defiant child might earn her rewards by coming home before curfew or completing homework without complaining.

Post the chart in a public place, like the refrigerator door, only if your child is proud and comfortable with that exposure. For a young child, give an award (or privilege) for each day's success. For an older child, chart the behavior for a week and mark each day's success with a sticker, star, or other physical reminder of progress. Once a goal is reached (say, five gold-star days out of seven), celebrate success with a big reward like a family outing.

In one family, a child who is working on his hostile, angry behavior is charted for controlling his anger during the day's three trouble spots: before school, after school, and bedtime. He earns a star for each time period during which he speaks courteously to family members. He is allowed to express his opinions and to disagree, but he loses his star if he screams, calls names, or speaks rudely.

Improving attitude problems, like rudeness or fighting with siblings, is usually more successful if you offer immediate rewards for positive behavior. For example, if your daughter pours a glass of milk without spilling, she could earn a token, like a poker chip, to save up for a reward.

COPING WITH YOUR OWN STRESS

As you work on helping your child improve her behavior, don't forget to take good care of yourself as well. As the parent of a demanding child, you need your strength—both physical and emotional.

• Visualize a bright future for your family and for your child as an adult. Don't waste time fantasizing about your child turning into a different, easier person; focus on the real child at her best.

"I try to picture Sam going off to college," says the mother of an energetic, impulsive, socially outgoing child. "He'd be in heaven with people everywhere, fun things to do, keeping busy, busy, busy. I can't imagine he would have any anxiety or homesickness, like I experienced when I went to college."

• Give yourself a break. When your responsibilities as a parent weigh you down, hire a sitter and go out for an elegant dinner.

• Be on the alert for warning signs of burnout.

• Meditate. Pray. Whatever your choice, take time for a calming, nourishing form of relaxation that helps you rebuild your strength and equilibrium.

• Don't forget to laugh. When your demanding child does something silly, allow yourself to laugh. Laughter is therapeutic for you *and* for your child; during tense times, she may not see enough of your laughter.

• Reach out to others for help. Avoid isolation. Be honest with parents of your demanding child's playmates. Most will cooperate and give your child a chance, if you show you're aware of her difficulties and are working actively to improve them.

If you are fortunate enough to have a positive relationship with in-laws and other family members, make use of them. Share your concerns about your demanding child. Ask family members for advice—even if you don't have to follow all of it, they'll be honored to be asked. Your mother-in-law may tell you that when your wife was four, she behaved exactly like your daughter.

• Delegate. Others can provide some care for your demanding child. Others can share your burdens by listening or counseling. And remember that the person to whom you'll ultimately delegate the effort and worry will be your challenging child herself, when she's older and wiser and eager to take on the responsibility.

PASSING THE BATON TO YOUR DEMANDING CHILD

As your child grows, she will take over more and more of this role. Your role will gradually evolve from hands-on manager to that of mentor and consultant.

The children described at the beginning of this chapter were already applying to themselves the techniques outlined in this chapter. They were coping with high energy, impulsiveness, and anger on their own.

As you teach your child to recognize her own sense of building anger or out-of-control energy, you're paving the way for her to govern her own behavior.

You can teach her to talk to herself about her feelings: "I'm starting to get upset. I'd better take a break."

You can teach her to count to ten or breathe deeply.

She can recognize when she needs to leave the room or give herself a change of scene in some way.

She can learn to assess whether she really wants what she's asking for, or whether she's just stuck in a pattern.

Your challenging child will always be challenging, and she will always be your child. But someday, she will be an adult, an independent person who is capable of doing for herself many of the things you do for her now. Eventually, she'll be able to explain her temperament and her behavior to others in the positive ways you've taught her. She'll be doing for herself the things you do for her now. She'll be able to:

- understand,
- respect,
- comfort,
- inspire,
- limit, and
- forgive herself.

Whenever you talk to your demanding child in a way that focuses on the behavior at hand, rather than her inadequacies, you make her more open to ways of solving problems and managing on her own. Whenever you teach her new skills and ways of coping, you're giving her the strength she needs to manage on her own in the future.

There may be times when you feel like a policeman or jailer, especially when your child is being particularly difficult. When things improve, you'll feel more like a parole officer.

But as your child grows older, you'll get promoted. If you do your job right, you get promoted from policeman to teacher, from foreman to supervisor, from boss to consultant. You become less of a benign dictator and more of a trusted advisor—and, ultimately, a loving parent and good friend of your adult challenging child.

◈ 7 ◈

Beyond Tantrums:
Understanding and Helping the
Unusually Angry Child

Alexa's kindergarten class is painting. Supplies are limited, so the five-year-olds have to wait their turn. In groups of four, the children take their places at the easels until it's time for the next group.

Alexa is beside herself with eagerness. But somehow, there's a mixup and she misses her turn. Desperate for the chance to paint, she tries to tell the teacher, who is distracted and doesn't hear her.

Finally, Alexa's patience snaps. She stamps her foot and knocks over chairs. "I want to paint!" she screams. "No fair! I want to paint!"

At eight, Kevin has already been suspended from school several times for punching other children. At home, he smashes dishes when his mother reprimands him or denies him a privilege. For Kevin, hitting, punching, and breaking are his standard repertoire. Anger and aggression are becoming his fundamental way of responding to the

129

world. When he wants something, he uses his anger to get it.

Alexa and Kevin are two angry children who display two very different kinds of anger. Throughout this book, we've discussed anger as one category of the demanding child. It may be difficult to manage, but it's a normal temperament trait.

Alexa's anger falls into this category. Her kindergarten outburst, though disruptive, was an example of anger serving its healthy purpose. Something urgently needed attention. Other methods weren't getting her anywhere. Only a display of noisy intensity served to get the job done.

But for some children, like Kevin, anger is no longer serving a useful purpose. It is severe, destructive, and all-consuming. It becomes a defining quality of their interactions. When a child who already has a disposition toward anger and intense emotion also experiences circumstances that make anger more intense, or more difficult to control, we see a child who is unusually angry. This chapter is about this unusual anger, as distinguished from the temperament trait we've been discussing.

Of all the categories of demanding behavior in this book, anger is the most distressing for parents. Certainly, a highly energetic child is a handful. An impulsive or stubborn child can strain the patience of the best of parents. But anger is upsetting, and the angry child's tantrums and expressions of rage are particularly worrisome to parents.

And when that anger is extreme—like Kevin's—

it generates even more concern from parents. It can impinge on a child's relationships and future in negative ways. That's why we've singled out this trait for special treatment. This chapter will investigate the more severe manifestations of anger: the unusually angry child, what contributes to that anger, and how parents can help pull an angry child back from the brink.

Anger is a universal human experience. We all have experienced the racing pulse, feeling of heightened tension, the urge to kick or smash.

Children, of course, are equipped with all the mechanisms necessary to produce and display anger. They display it when they are frustrated, thwarted, or ignored. When these outbursts are intense and noisy, we call them tantrums.

Because children are by definition less mature than adults, less capable of applying wisdom and experience to intense emotions, their anger is often expressed inappropriately.

Sometimes, however, a child's hostility is severe enough to warrant its own psychiatric diagnosis: Oppositional Defiant Disorder (ODD) or, in the case of serious aggression and misbehavior, Conduct Disorder (CD).

In this chapter, we won't deal with specific diagnoses (just as we didn't diagnose Attention Deficit Hyperactive Disorder), but we'll look at what is going on with the child who is unusually angry, unusually intense, aggressive, or hostile—and what approaches are most effective.

First, let's look at what anger is biologically, what its purposes are, and why it can create severe problems for the individual and the community.

THE CASE FOR ANGER

Without the capacity to feel and express anger, human beings might not have survived. In our early millennia, predators would take advantage of us and probably, quite literally, have us for breakfast. We'd be unable to scare away our enemies or threaten our rivals. We'd be incapable of motivating ourselves to take vigorous, immediate action to fix some danger or right an injustice.

Fortunately, we possess structures in our brain that interpret threats, release epinephrine (also known as adrenaline), and set into motion the typical body processes of anger: the rise in blood pressure and heart rate, the tensing of muscles, the raising of hackles and hair follicles, the baring of teeth, the tightening of vocal cords.

All this activity leaves us in a state of heightened alertness and readiness. It has a valuable role in keeping us alive, and that accounts for the preservation of these functions and reactions into the present.

In contemporary life, of course, saber-toothed tigers are less evident. Our need to engage in hand-to-hand combat is minimal, or so one would hope. Yet we still gain benefits from our ability to experience the emotions that accompanied our more hair-triggered past.

When we've been wronged, it's natural to feel angry at the guilty party. It would be abnormal to feel no surge of rage at someone who steals your car, runs off with your spouse, or spreads false rumors about you.

Anger can motivate us. That surge of epinephrine that tells us, Act! Just Do It! can get us launched, out of our rut and toward solutions to our problems.

And anger can get results. If we have been treated shabbily, and our polite efforts for redress are ignored, sometimes a display of ferocity gets attention. The red face, tensed shoulders, and shaking voice show opponents that we are serious indeed. It shows we mean business.

The action that we take as a result of the anger serves two purposes: It reduces the immediate tension, so our body returns to normal, and it may serve to alter the situation that caused the anger. Whether we've chased an enemy away from the prehistoric water hole, or managed to get our money back from a malfunctioning vending machine, our anger has helped solve the problem.

Our capacity for anger represents passion. It's a mark of the extent to which we care about things. We would all be robots if this emotion were completely eliminated from our lives.

Because of the importance of anger from an evolutionary standpoint, our bodies are equipped to display this emotion externally. These outward signs of anger constitute an important means of communication. When we see someone with a red face, clenched teeth and fists, shoulders tensed, hissing breath, shaking, we think, "Whhooaa! Better back off!"

. . . AND THE CASE AGAINST

There is, of course, a dark side to this basic emotion. Like fear, it can protect us on one hand and cripple us on the other.

When anger takes over our lives, and becomes difficult or impossible to channel and guide and control when necessary, it becomes our master, rather than our servant.

The instant fury that served us in primitive settings leads us astray in modern life. Our bodies rally to frighten predators or attack enemies with our fists. But the kind of threat we experience in the modern world is less immediate. We end up waving our fists at bad drivers or cursing the Internal Revenue Service. We don't succeed in chasing away any wild beasts, and we're left with our anger.

Or if we express it directly, it's inappropriate and destructive. If we're competing with a rival for a date to the prom, or for a coveted promotion at work, smacking the enemy over the head with a club is unlikely to further our goals.

As if we didn't have enough trouble managing the kind of anger that comes to us almost spontaneously, we have the capacity—thanks to our higher brain functions—to dwell on our anger.

Despite its primitive origins, anger is intimately linked to our higher mental functions. We use those functions to control and manage anger, and we also use them to heighten and cultivate (and justify) anger. Thus, we make ourselves even more angry than we would be if we were lower creatures whose anger existed solely in the primitive areas of the brain.

So the angry child, like the angry adult, doesn't just seethe and explode and sputter and hit. He also broods. He justifies his anger. He works himself up over the frustration or threat or need that makes him angry.

In this way, we are all betrayed by the very mental capacities that we could be using to manage and control our anger. When we use memory and imagination to feed our anger, it gets worse. And usually, after we release the anger in an outburst, the cause of our anger still remains.

To make matters worse, extreme anger is associated with a range of health problems, including heart disease and digestive problems.

And so we're left with our clenched teeth, our elevated blood pressure, and our enemies still taunting us.

What do we do with all this rage?

One school of thought advocates the release of anger, and the reduction of all this harmful pressure, through the extravagant expression of rage. Because anger is such an integral part of our physical being, and because the unrelieved buildup of anger can be unhealthful and destructive, some students of human behavior have viewed anger as a form of internal pressure that requires release.

After all, the total denial and repression of anger is hardly healthy and constructive. Denying our unhappiness and feeling ashamed of our legitimate feelings is neither healthy nor constructive. We should express all our feelings, including our negative ones. We should recall injustices, confront those who have wronged us, bellow our rage, pummel punching bags, and experience a cleansing release of tension.

We should, in other words, throw a good tantrum.

However, studies have shown that in most cases the intense expression of anger through body language, shouting, throwing, and breaking actually *increases* the sense of misery, frustration and low self-esteem that promoted it in the first place; so does dwelling on anger, fanning its flames, wallowing in it and brooding in our tents.

Anger needs to be addressed and accepted as a feeling—an indication of unhappiness and dissatisfaction, a warning that some need hasn't been met. But it should not be approached as a force that needs releasing, like a boil to be lanced.

The unrestrained expression of anger does the following:

• It actually increases stress in the angry person. It makes the angry person *more* angry.

• Anger produces anger in the person at whom it is directed. Whether it's two third-graders escalating a shoving match in the schoolyard or two drivers cutting each other off in busy traffic, each participant's display of rage heightens the rage of the other.

• It traps the angry person at one emotional state and prevents him from being open to more satisfying emotions. The very qualities of anger that make it stimulating and energizing also make it seductive and difficult to give up.

• Anger interferes with the ability to find solutions that might actually ease the angry person's suffering. A frustrated child who can't tie his shoes, and yanks so hard that he breaks the laces, is venting his frustration, but he's not learning how to tie shoes. The husband who responds to stress in his marriage by raging at his wife is less likely to be able to take action to improve the relationship.

• It interferes with intimacy and alienates friends, neighbors, family, children, and community. It drives away the affection and support that the angry person so desperately needs.

• In children, anger often masks an array of hurts and anxieties, making them difficult to recognize.

• It gets the angry person in trouble with authority figures like bosses and law enforcement.

• It leads to violence against people and property.

So naturally, we don't want our demanding children to go through life in the grip of uncontrollable anger. We worry about the impact of all that hostility on their relationships with friends and on their ability to get an education. We worry about how to cope with their anger at home, and its impact on other family members. And most of all, we sense that the extremely angry child is, to some extent, an unhappy child.

What can we do when our demanding child is unusually angry or hostile? First, let's look at some of the factors that contribute to unusual anger in children.

CAUSES OF ANGER IN CHILDREN

Biological origins or predispositions

The systematic study of biology and human aggression is fairly recent. Through the use of the insights and technologies described in Chapter 2, medical researchers are learning more about the causes of unusual aggression and possible ways to treat it.

Some findings:

- Head injury and prenatal drug or alcohol influence can be related to aggressive behavior.
- A pattern of low serotonin activity in the brain is linked to aggressive, antisocial, and impulsive behaviors.
- Males are more likely than females to be unusually aggressive or impulsive.
- Mental retardation or psychosis can contribute to difficulties with impulse control.
- Attention Deficit Hyperactive Disorder can translate into impulsive and defiant behavior.
- Unusually low autonomic nervous system activity, as measured by heart rate and skin conductivity, have been associated with aggressive and criminal behavior.

Considerable research is being conducted into the use of antidepressants and other medications to reduce impulsivity and aggression. Both adults and children who are prone to extreme aggression, especially of an impulsive nature, seem better able to control their impulses under medication. This research is shedding light on the biological mechanisms of anger and aggression. Ultimately, however, most treatment of angry children will rely on modifying behavior through consistent discipline and the building of skills and habits that promote anger control.

Family experiences

If the capacity for angry feelings and aggressive behavior are part of our biological heritage, it is not the only cause. There are circumstances, settings, and family dynamics that make it more likely a child will have difficulty controlling anger.

• Separation and loss. The death of a parent, divorce, or severe disruptions between the child and his attachments to loved ones can result in sadness and grief which children often express through anger and misbehavior.

Sam's early years were marked by frequent separations before he was adopted by a stable family at the age of five.

Although Sam was bright, friendly, and energetic, his early losses left him with painful feelings that flared easily into defiance and anger, especially when his desires and impulses were checked by his parents.

At first, Sam's parents were upset and bewildered by his rage. But over time, they began to see it as the outward sign of grief, and to reach through it with the affection and support Sam so desperately needed.

• Abuse or neglect. A child who has been hurt may lash out in an attempt to hurt back. A child whose physical needs are neglected may use inappropriate means to try to fill those needs.

• Detachment or emotional neglect from parents. Children who have not been able to form a close attachment may have reduced empathy for others, and reduced ability to control their impulses.

• Patterns of angry expression or violence within the home. Children who grow up in families that behave violently learn aggressive behavior, even if the adult aggression isn't aimed directly at the child.

Cultural influences

Different cultural traditions view the expression of anger differently. If you jostle someone on the street, your offense will get different responses in Tokyo and New York. And the expression of anger varies within subcultures; a vigorous difference of opinion sounds one way in a Quaker meetinghouse and another on a street in South Central Los Angeles. And within each cultural setting, there is variation among families in the way anger is viewed and expressed.

Clearly, although anger is a universal biological function, it is expressed differently according to culture and experience. As children grow and learn, they express anger in ways that are defined by their culture.

In contemporary society, powerful influences glorify rage and aggression, especially for men and boys. Games, movies, entertainment, and sports often show violence as exciting, and as a sign of maturity and manliness.

And in a competitive culture like ours, anger is intimately tied to issues of power.

To show inappropriate anger is to lose control, to throw off all cultural restraints and revert to one's basic instinctual self. Yet rage, or the threat of rage, is a way of exerting or keeping power. Adults, from lawyers to voters to cheated customers, do this. Violent men use their anger—real or potential—to maintain power over wives. Parents threaten anger and violence to keep children in line. And children may learn that their rages frighten their parents.

Finally, an essential element of anger is learned. If we habitually express anger without restraint, if we're encouraged to "vent" our feelings, ignoring their consequences, we're more likely to do so, and the behavior can become habitual.

Children can develop habits of angry expression. They may persist in using violent or aggressive behaviors because there's a payoff. Whatever the causes of Kevin's anger, for example, there is an element of habit to his behavior.

If anger can be learned, it can be unlearned. If displays of anger and aggression can become habitual, then other, more positive ways of expressing strong feelings can become habitual as well.

Anger can in most cases be managed, redirected, and channeled in constructive directions.

The key is to redirect the anger while still letting this ancient emotion do what it is intended to do: getting us to focus on a need or problem, and communicating to others how serious we are.

START WITH YOUR OWN ANGER

Children can be exasperating at times, and demanding children can be more so. But a constantly angry child who seems on the attack all the time can stimulate feelings of rage in parents. It's difficult to be constructive about your child's angry behavior if your own is erupting like a volcano. Your best bet is to step back a bit and examine your own angry feelings, then work back to what you can do to help your angry child.

• Think about your own experiences with anger. As we discussed in Chapter 3, our early experiences with emotions affect how we judge them and respond to them today.

• When your child is angry, try not to add fuel to the flames by adding your own anger to the mix. You can convey your displeasure at your child's misdeeds. If you're getting really mad, say so, but express yourself calmly: "I'm feeling angry with you because I told you that vase was breakable."

• Focus on solutions to the problem. If your impulsive child grabs a can of soft drink from the refrigerator, drops it on the floor, then opens it with an explosion of foam all over the floor, try to resist displaying your exasperation. It's better to say something like, "Let's get this mess cleaned up."

• Give yourself a time-out if you're really upset.

• If you are under unusual stress that might make you particularly short-tempered, give fair warning to your child. If you've been pulled in three directions at work, if your desk is piling with urgent work and you are bringing papers home every night, you may be more likely to overreact and lose your temper at your child. When that happens, explain that your bad mood is caused by something else, and not by your child.

• Apologize to your child if you express anger in a way that you know is excessive. Suppose you give your child money to buy milk at the store, and he spends the change on baseball cards instead of returning it to you as you'd asked. You explode in rage because it's the end of the month and you need to save every penny.

After you've calmed down a bit, you can say, "I really lost my temper there. I shouldn't have yelled at you. I had a right to be upset that you spent the money, but it wasn't right to yell."

• Calm yourself with self-talk: "This is pretty annoying, but I can handle it. He's the kid, I'm the adult. It's just a spill; it will clean up."

HELPING YOUR CHILD WITH HIS ANGER

• Contain aggressive behavior. Don't let it continue unchecked. If your three-year-old pounces on a playmate, he needs to be restrained.

• Avoid rewarding angry or aggressive displays. Take away the incentives: Make sure that blowing up doesn't win an argument, settle scores, or yield lots of attention.

• Remove the element of anger from punishment. Rely on impersonal limits when possible. Instead of screaming when you find your four-year-old drawing on the living room wall, issue an appropriate punishment.

• Emphasize etiquette. There's a good reason for timeless rules about courtesy. They keep minor annoyances from building into major ones. And they help depersonalize the ordinary irritants of daily life. If someone's grocery cart bumps into yours at the store, that person usually says, "Oops, sorry." And you usually smile and say, "No problem." You don't put your wounded inner self on the line with every interaction.

• Teach assertiveness, and how it's different from aggressiveness. Standing up for one's rights in a calm manner is an essential skill. It focuses on finding fair solutions to the problems that provoke anger, rather than using rage as a threat or a punishment.

• Be specific about what behaviors are acceptable and which ones are not. Instead of telling your kids, "Stop fighting!" or "Play nicely," say, "Remember the rule about name-calling."

• Teach your child conflict resolution skills, or have him learn them in a workshop or class setting. These skills include how to express displeasure appropriately, how to listen, how to negotiate a solution. Role playing may be used to practice these techniques.

As you try to get your child to solve problems without aggression, you may have to demonstrate the process first, then encourage your child take over the responsibility himself.

1. State the conflict. "I see two children who want to use the swing. What are some things we might do?"

2. Seek possible solutions. Have the children toss out ideas. They might include, "Let *me* use the swing," "Play another game," or "Take turns."

3. Agree on the best solution. "Taking turns means two kids can have fun even when there's only one swing."

4. Apply the solution and see how it works.

5. Praise the skill with which the children resolved their conflict. "You kids did a good job of solving the problem about the swing today."

• Foster empathy. Remind children of what happens when people are violent. Point out what victims feel. Model empathic behavior yourself, by showing concern for the needs and feelings of others. When your child reads stories that make feelings come alive, or when he cares for a pet, he's developing empathy.

Beware, also, of entertainment and cultural influences that undermine empathy. That's a risk that comes with a lot of violent or aggressive entertainment. The audience in some sporting events, such as hockey or professional wrestling, for example, is encouraged to cut themselves off from feelings of concern for the players who are hurt, or pretending to be.

• Don't encourage your child to "ventilate" anger by punching a pretend person or throwing darts at a picture of his enemy. It's fine for your child to talk about his anger and who he's mad at. But a dramatic acting out of violence toward the enemy actually prolongs the anger. It's better to blow off anger by playing music, by drawing a "mad" picture, or running around the block. However, if your child consistently expresses anger by hitting others, he may need the opportunity to pound on a punching bag or pillow as a better alternative.

• Children vary in how they release tension. One child feels calmer after hitting a punching bag, but another just gets angrier and angrier. Guide your child toward the stress reliever that works best for him.

• Reinforce the idea that a peaceful solution has rewards—it isn't just something you're making your child do. Demonstrate how negotiating results in good outcomes. Sharing means everybody gets something. Taking turns results in fun and pleasant feelings. Cooperation is its own reward.

• Seek out role models for your child who are

peaceful, who have authority and dignity and are respected, but who are nonviolent and nonaggressive. Some religious and political leaders fill this bill, as do some sports heroes who behave with skill and civility.

• Limit your angry child's exposure to violent entertainment, including television, movies, musical lyrics, and video games. These media often glorify aggression and the use of force to solve difficulties. A steady diet of this entertainment appears to increase aggression in children.

• When your child expresses anger appropriately (meaning perhaps loudly, but not violently), listen respectfully to the feelings and words.

• Praise your child's efforts and progress toward managing his anger.

• An angry, disruptive child may be responding to negative attention. Don't put on a flamboyant display of your own every time your child loses control of his temper.

WHEN TO SEEK HELP

Parents of angry children often need the support of a professional who treats family issues and childhood aggression. Often a therapist can help identify the hurt that childhood anger so often masks. In addition, therapy provides further tools for helping parents manage aggressive behavior.

The very angry child should be evaluated by a professional if:

- His anger causes you to become, or fear you will become, violent toward him.
- He is big enough to hurt you and is physically abusive to you.
- He fights constantly and hurts other children.
- His aggression seems to be increasing, or not improving despite your best efforts.
- He demonstates cruelty to animals or serious destructiveness toward property.

◇ **8** ◇

Trouble Spots:
Helping Your Demanding Child Cope With
Difficult Settings

Ellen is an ten-year-old whose energy meshes well with the rest of her athletic family. In her home, noise and physical activity are accepted and celebrated, and Ellen's need to be physically active is seen as perfectly normal.

School, however, is a different story. Ellen's fourth-grade teacher is conscientious, traditional, and quiet. She expects children to sit still and pay attention. Ellen is not coping well with this environment. She squirms at her desk and calls out answers without waiting to be called on. She asks for permission to go to the bathroom. She taps her pencil constantly. Her teacher says her behavior is distracting the class.

Ellen's parents do not view her as a demanding child when she's at home with them. But in school, her high energy is viewed as a problem.

Greg, on the other hand, exhausts his parents. Persistent and insatiable, he needs constant attention. He doesn't enjoy being alone or playing independently, and when he's bored, he becomes sullen and negative.

But Gregory thrives at school. He actually loves Mondays, because it means the beginning of a busy week with lots of challenges and people to share them with.

Greg is in his element at school; Ellen is in hers at home.

Demanding children react differently in different settings, as do all children. But their behavior is more variable because they depend more than other children do on structure and limits to frame their behavior.

Their behavior may be worse at different times of the day, among different friends, and during certain tasks. Exactly what setting gives your child trouble is an individual matter. But there are some common trouble spots that create difficulties for many demanding children. This chapter is about identifying and coping with those situations.

MANAGING SETTING: THE BIG PICTURE

You and your child will be better able to cope with difficult settings if you can recognize them, plan for them, work around them, and/or help your child manage her temperament when she's in them.

By now you know what activities and settings are difficult for your child. You've probably noticed, too, that your child handles these situations better at certain times and worse at others. For many children, the hour just before dinner is the most likely to produce explosions and tantrums. For high-energy children, there is nothing worse than vacations, where you go straight from a long car trip to sitting in a restaurant.

When possible, match activities to your child's rhythms of energy and fatigue. Children handle stressful situations better when they are feeling rested, strong, and capable. If your angry child is a morning person, schedule playdates in the morning, not the afternoon when her temper is more likely to fray.

Your persistent daughter may be able to handle a series of errands more easily after her nap: For her, transitions are energy consumers. Make sure she's in peak condition when you try to get her to accept frequent changes of scene.

The time element is important, also, in how long a child can handle a difficult setting. There's not too much you can do about the length of the school day, but you can keep other activities short. Trips to the museum and visits to friends' homes are open-ended and can be trimmed so your child will be able to leave before she is worn out.

Those situations that are harder to cut short, such as religious services, movies, or air travel, need to be kept to a minimum and planned with care.

EVERYDAY TROUBLE SPOTS

For most children, home is the most comfortable setting of all. Yet it's in the daily routines that many demanding children show their true colors. And many, like Greg, save their most challenging behavior for home.

DRESSING

SITUATION: Your persistent child hates the way you've braided her hair. She says you've done it wrong, and demands that you redo it. You try again, and she still hates it.

WHAT TO DO: Persistent children easily escalate small dissatisfactions into full-fledged battles. When this happens, remember that the crisis really isn't about braids. It's about a tendency to get stuck, and not knowing how to get unstuck.

Redoing braids once is fine, but repeating the cycle is a waste of energy and goodwill. You can be understanding, but you need to be firm: "I know you want your braids right, and it's hard for you to stop asking me to do them over. But we're not getting anywhere. You have a choice: Leave them as they are, or comb them out and wear your hair the way you're comfortable."

Other dressing situations generate ideal opportunities for similar locked-in behavior, especially about not liking certain clothes. There's also dawdling, outright refusals, or insisting on wearing the same thing for seven days straight.

• Energetic toddlers and preschoolers either won't hold still or insist on scurrying off to play before they're dressed. Try cornering your child in a room without distractions. You may have to dress her in the bathroom with the door closed to prevent escape.

• Watch out for frustrations that trigger tantrums in preschoolers: buttons that don't button, shoes that are hard to lace, or zippers that don't zip.

• Clothing brings out a whole array of power issues. Conflicts can lead to defiance and anger. Joshua insists on wearing shorts long into the fall weather. His mother hates to see his bare legs heading out to the bus stop on a brisk morning. Her arguments don't have any effect. Natural consequences don't have much effect, since Joshua would rather freeze to death than admit at the end of the day that he was cold.

Joshua's parents have two choices in this situation: First, they can redefine the shorts issue as a Nonessential Priority, as we outlined in Chapter 6. They could say, "Okay, Josh. You've convinced us that whether you wear shorts is more important to you than it is to us. You can make your own decision." Joshua will probably survive having cold legs, even though the neighbors might disapprove.

Their second choice is to negotiate a sensible rule. They could settle on a temperature, say, 50 degrees, as the cut-off for shorts weather. Joshua could look at the thermometer and at the newspaper weather forecast and respond to that, not to his parents. Leaving the decision in neutral, measurable territory takes the power element out of it.

Mealtime

Food and mealtimes present difficulties for demanding chidren because they have trouble sitting still, have trouble waiting, and have a tendency to be hostile or to complain about the food. These are all behaviors which do not make for a pleasant dining experience.

It's easy for mealtime to become an arena for struggles that are more about power and independence than they are about nourishing the body and sharing a pleasant time.

SITUATION: You're trying to get the family to sit down for dinner, but your persistent seven-year-old child is resisting. He wants to finish his television program before he joins the family. When he drags himself into the kitchen, he complains about the menu. He hates the kind of chicken with bones in it. You ask him to eat his vegetables and he eats a tiny piece of one green bean. Soon, you and the rest of the family are losing your patience and your appetite.

WHAT TO DO: Your son is showing what's called negative persistence—a negative, impossible-to-please mind-set that persistent children often display. You can't make your child like the food, or feel cheerful, but you can expect him to adhere to basic rules of civility.

If you think the issue is really about the food, suggest that your child help select the menu for the next family dinner. If he's involved in selecting

and preparing the meal, he may not be so oppositional.

But ultimately, he is behaving rudely and violat-
ing basic etiquette at the table, so he needs specific
rules, with specific consequences. He may benefit
from a star chart that tracks the times he gets
through a meal pleasantly and without complaint.

Other suggestions for demanding children and
meals:

• Keep meals and table settings simple if you
have an impulsive child who spills. Use unbreak-
able plates and cups, and serve her drink in small
amounts until she gains more self-control. A child
whose actions are awkward is not being disobedient when she spills. But she still needs help getting
through a meal more gracefully.

• Persistent children may demand the same food
every day. Within reason, food jags are not usually
harmful to children. If you insist on a rigid inter-
pretation of the four basic food groups three times
a day, your child may increase her resistance.

• Persistent, insatiable children can be relentless
in their demand for junk food and treats. Be firm
about the rules. Set a negotiated rule about treats
or sugar foods and post it on the refrigerator if necessary. From then on, it's the rule, not a personal
power struggle.

• Use a lighted candle as a visual reminder of the
formal part of a family meal. Expect good mealtime
behavior until the candle is blown out and your
child can leave the table.

Bedtime

Probably this is the most difficult time of day for demanding children, with the possible exception of those high-energy kids who have been going full blast all day and fall asleep instantly at the same time every night. Those are the easy ones; you simply let them run down, point them toward their pajamas, and tuck them in. They're asleep before you can turn out the lights.

More common is a situation like Nathan's.

SITUATION: Six-year-old Nathan seems to draw energy from physical activity, growing ever more active and noisy as the evening wears on. His mother—understandably—gets worn out and is ready to drop by eight o'clock. Nathan's father tries valiantly to wear him down by roughhousing with him during the evening. Soon everyone except Nate is tired.

WHAT TO DO: Nathan, like many high-energy kids, needs an evening schedule that will help him shift from overdrive into neutral. He may need a later bedtime than children with less pep, but it should be a regular time each evening. He needs to start the wind-down early, with quieter play, perhaps a bedtime snack, and a warm bath. Since all these are pleasant activities, Nathan can probably be lured from one activity to the next, ending with his favorite bedtime stories.

Bedtime can also be difficult for children who are defiant and intense. Outbursts and tantrums often occur. Bedtime is a perfect opportunity for testing, for refusing to cooperate, and for pushing the envelope of parental tolerance. Outbursts and tantrums frequently occur just when parents may have the least patience and energy to handle them.

And persistent kids are the ones who genuinely hate having to stop what they're doing. They may take longer to wake up in the morning, and they take longer to want to sleep at night. That's especially true for children who wake up from a nap crabby and out of sorts.

• Allow enough time for a bedtime routine. For very young children, that routine may involve soothing baths, several bedtime stories, lullabies, and hugs. For older children, it may involve a television program, or a play session with quiet toys.

• Do give your child advance warning as bedtime approaches. Remind her at intervals that it will soon be time for bed.

• Persistent children always want one more story, one more drink of water, one more hug. Set reasonable limits, tell your child what they are, and adhere to them. You might say, "You've had your water. You've had your three stories. One more hug, and then goodnight."

FRIENDSHIP AND SOCIAL LIFE

Demanding children frequently have difficulty forging friendships because they have trouble controlling their bodies and their actions. They may find it hard to follow rules in group games. They may be aggressive and angry when they lose, or when they don't get their way. They may have trouble sharing and taking turns, and they may be relentless in their need to be the center of attention.

All of these are traits that can discourage friendship, yet all of them are behaviors that can be changed or at least modified. Children need to learn social skills. It's not enough to toss them into a social setting and "let them work it out themselves." That might work with some kids who are easygoing and naturally cooperative, but demanding children need more from us.

Impulsive and high-energy kids sometimes miss the lessons and the cues other children pick up naturally, because they've been blasting full speed ahead and don't stop for subtleties.

Demanding children benefit when they can identify specific skills that help them enter a group, ask for attention, negotiate, and solve problems.

Persistent children who are insatiable often have trouble with limits and boundaries. They may have trouble obeying rules, taking turns, limiting their own need for attention, and respecting space (whether in a sandbox or in a friend's home).

SITUATION: Your six-year-old son is spending the afternoon at the home of a friend the same age. The phone rings, and it's the friend's mother. She says in a stiff voice, "I'm afraid the boys aren't getting along. They started fighting over the controller on the video game, and David hit Jared and gave him a bloody nose. I think David needs to go home."

WHAT TO DO: First, you apologize and express sympathy for Jared's bloody nose. You pick up your son and ask him to apologize to Jared. You explain to his mother that you are working with David on his aggressive behavior. You express the hope that at a later date, the boys might play together again.

When you get David home, you remind him that it's essential to solve problems without hitting. You point out that his action hurt Jared, and resulted in an abrupt end to the visit. You work with David on the social and anger management skills we've outlined earlier. And finally, you remind your son that even though he made a mistake today, he's a basically good kid who will learn to do better.

Other social problems of demanding children:

• Persistent, insatiable children sometimes annoy their peers with constant demands for attention. Stephanie needs to be the center of attention at all times. She constantly asks her friends for praise and admiration. "Isn't mine pretty?" is woven into her conversations. When she and her friends play fantasy games, Stephanie needs to be the princess or the mommy every time or she becomes upset.

There may be other issues in Stephanie's experience, like fear of inadequacy or loss of a loved one, that make her anxious and needy. Whatever the cause, however, she needs to modify her behavior.

Stephanie needs to understand two things: first, that her behavior makes her a less pleasant companion, and that she will benefit from changing it.

And she needs to view insatiable attention-grabbing behavior like other kinds of greed. Most kids don't want to play with someone who won't share. Encourage Stephanie to offer attention to others, as well as seek it for herself. She might precede her statements with praise for another child: "I like your picture. Do you like mine?" She and her friends might set up a plan to take turns sharing the spotlight. When Stephanie becomes used to the idea that attention comes and goes and there's plenty for everyone, she may relax her grip on the need to be on stage.

• Demanding children often have trouble controlling their behavior at parties, as do less challenging children. High-energy and impulsive children may become wild; angry and persistent children may fight or refuse to cooperate in games.

• When your demanding child is the birthday girl, she may have trouble being a gracious hostess. She may have trouble moving from one game or activity to another.

When she opens presents, she may find fault with the gifts or seem ungrateful. Children who have trouble with transitions, in particular, get stuck. They open one present and want to stop and play with it, ignoring the remaining gifts and the circle of watchful party guests.

If present opening is a problem, you have several options:

• Keep the party very small so the number of gifts is small.
• Save the gifts to open after the party, making sure to send thank you notes to the guests.
• Teach your child to smile and say "thank you,"

even if she's not sure she likes something. Practice with her before the party.

AWAY FROM THE NEST

Away from home, you'll need to learn how to be your demanding child's advocate in the outside world. Whether you're talking with your child's teacher or coach, or with relatives or neighbors, you'll need to draw on your positive vocabulary to discuss her temperament with others.

At the same time, you'll need to be tactful in how you do this. You want to advocate without seeming to make excuses for your child's difficult behavior. Your job description is daunting: You'll serve as both her lawyer and her ambassador.

Day care and nursery school

Demanding children often do quite well when they enter nursery school. They experience less separation anxiety than more timid children, and they usually respond well to the opportunities for play and socializing.

However, nursery school can be the first time a demanding child has to conform to rules and expectations outside the home. For some children, the difficulty is controlling their anger, or learning to share with other children. For some high-energy children, it's something as basic as learning to sit still.

"Anthony's whole body goes all the time," his preschool teacher reported to his mother. "During circle, he gets on all fours and bucks like a bronco. He's much better when he's at the crayon table and he can do something with his hands."

Some suggestions:

• Discuss your child's temperament with the teacher, using positive language that focuses on your child's needs. You might say, "Anthony has a lot of physical energy. He might do better with circle time if he gets to run around just beforehand, or if he can hold a toy while he sits."

• Your demanding child may be enthusiastic about the idea of nursery school, but she'll still need support and reassurance if she is separating from you for the first time. You'll need to prepare her for the big day, discuss it in a positive way, and reassure her that you'll come back to pick her up at the end of the day. Even if your child seems confident about the new experience, you may want to make use of the transitional period many nursery schools offer, staying in the room with her for decreasing amounts of time over the first few days.

• Persistent children sometimes have difficulty leaving nursery school at the end of the day because they're so engrossed in what they're doing.

Try to involve the teacher in helping your child prepare for departure. She might remind your child ten minutes ahead of time that you'll be arriving soon. She could set a timer, and your child can watch as your arrival grows closer. She can help her finish up whatever she's working on so that she doesn't have to abandon a favorite project when you arrive. She might set out her coat and backpack ahead of time to make the end-of-day transition smoother.

School

School can be a challenging environment for demanding children for many reasons. School offers different settings, like the bus, the cafeteria, gym class, and recess, each with its own opportunity for difficult behavior.

Teachers must, of necessity, cater to a large group of children who have individual temperaments and personalities. There's no way that one teacher can tailor the entire curriculum and schedule to the specific needs of each child. You and your child will have to do some compromising and some coping.

Suggestions for the school setting:

• Be aware of your child's learning style. Some children learn best by hearing spoken information; others learn best by seeing a picture, a chart, or by visualizing the material. Still others—and high-energy children are often in this group—learn best by doing, by physically manipulating materials or objects or acting out events.

One third-grade teacher who is attuned to learning styles has a special way of involving her high-energy pupils who have trouble staying focused in class: Instead of asking them questions orally, she'll throw them a soft soccer ball. Taped to the ball is a note with the child's question printed on it. The child reads the note, throws the ball back, and answers the question.

• If your have a choice about where your child will attend school, you're ahead of the game. If possible, select a school and a program that will honor your child's individuality, while helping her grow and channel her challenging traits.

If your child is particularly energetic, for example, you'd seek a program that includes plenty of opportunity for movement, for physical learning, for hands-on activities. Beware of schools and particular teachers that focus almost exclusively on desk work and worksheets.

• If you are planning to enroll your child in a school, observe the class. Watch the children, not just the teacher. Are children like yours happy? Are they treated the way you'd like your child to be treated? Are children told clearly what to expect, and when to expect it? Persistent children who have trouble with transitions do better when this information is plainly presented.

• If you know the school and the teachers, pay attention to the fit between teacher and child. Many teachers are adept at dealing with different temperaments among their children, but some are more successful than others. Often the teachers who are marvelous with certain children don't have the right style for a demanding child.

• If you think a particular teacher would be best for your child or would not be a good choice, do let the school principal know—but do so diplomatically. Many school districts either forbid, or strongly discourage, parental requests for a certain popular teacher.

However, most principals and headmasters really do want to find the best setting for each child. You might write the principal a letter in which you explain what your child needs, without making unreasonable demands. It could say, "My son is generally well-behaved, but he needs structure and predictability to do his best. I'd like to ask you to take that into consideration when you make class assignments for next year."

• If your school allows tours or visits in the summer before the school year begins, take your child to see the building. The more you both know about the setting she'll be working in, the easier it will be for her to manage.

• The school bus can be a difficult setting for demanding children. It's a small, confined space, with several dozen children of varying ages, and minimal supervision as the driver concentrates on the road. High-energy children have trouble staying in their seats, and the intensity of the crowded setting can light the fuses of angry children.

If your child can't cope with the school bus setting, or if her experiences there set a negative tone for the rest of the day, consider driving her yourself or carpooling until she is more mature. Or, if she must ride the bus, enlist the driver's help in keeping her on track. The driver may arrange for her to sit in the front of the bus or assign her a seatmate.

• Communicate with your child's teacher. Let

her know about your child's temperament and learning style. Talk about temperament in a positive, but realistic way. You might say, "You might find that Aaron takes a while to settle down and concentrate on his work. Sometimes he gets so fidgety he distracts the other kids. He seems to manage better when his desk is off to the side of the room."

• Be tactful when you talk with your child's teacher. Remember that she has a whole classroom full of students, all with different temperaments, to manage and to teach. Avoid accusing her of neglecting your child's needs, even if you think she could be more attentive. Resist the temptation to complain, and instead focus on finding workable ways of meeting your child's needs.

• See if you can find time to volunteer in your child's classroom, either as a room parent or other volunteer. This allows you to get a better sense of the classroom dynamics, and also develop a sense of teamwork with your child's teacher.

• As you discuss temperament with your child, talk about her teacher's style and personality. Ask her how she can tell what the teacher is thinking or how she is reacting. Does she clench her shoulders or write on the blackboard more vigorously when she is becoming upset? You want your child to learn to read other people, and to be aware of their reactions to her behavior.

• Beware of the transition to junior high or middle school. When children switch from a single classroom and teacher to the secondary pattern of changing rooms and teachers each period, they often feel overwhelmed. Your demanding child may not be able to avoid seventh grade, but she can enter middle school or junior high with as much preparation and support as you can provide.

• Extracurricular activities, team sports, and group lessons share many of the stresses of the school setting. Your demanding child will benefit from these activities, and from the chance to hone her social skills and self-control.

However, it's important to consider the issue of fit between a demanding child and a coach or group leader. If the coach is not capable of working with your child's temperament, if he is harshly critical of your child, or does not provide enough structure or set reasonable limits on behavior, you may need to reconsider the activity.

Homework

• Be realistic about how efficiently and cooperatively your child will be able to buckle down to work on school assignments. It may not be possible for her to be as organized and cheerful as you might like.

• High-energy children really do need some play time after school before doing homework if they've been sitting in the classroom all day.

• High-energy kids will probably squirm while they study. They may not look anything like the fantasy image of a well-groomed child sitting properly in a desk chair, with the desk lamp in just the right position.

"My son does most of his studying dangling from something," says a mother. "He's either hanging off the edge of his bed or falling out of his chair. I could make an issue of him sitting quietly at his desk, but for the time being it's okay with me that he's actually getting the work done."

• Angry children sometimes use schoolwork as an opportunity for tense explosions. If your child resists homework and doing well in school, you'll have to devise a way to get the power struggle out of the equation while still retaining your adult authority. Ask your child's teacher for a three-way conference, with you, your child and the teacher working on joint goals.

Eating out

Restaurants are a challenging setting for most demanding children. All the difficulties involved in at-home meals are present, plus the public setting that makes the child's negative behavior so stressful for parents.

• If your child is incapable of behaving reasonably well, postpone dining out, at least in formal settings, until she is more mature.

• Family-friendly settings are usually best for young, demanding children. You can't go wrong at a fast-food restaurant that has a kiddie playground. However, don't *always* play it safe. As time goes by, you'll want to try more challenging dining situations to give your child practice with self-control, etiquette, and courtesy.

• If the waiting area in your restaurant has video games or amusements, your child may have difficulty leaving the video game to head for the table. Prepare her in advance about what's going to happen and when.

• Prepare a survival kit for your child while you wait for the meal to be served. Fidgety kids need something for their hands to be doing while they're waiting. Crayons, paper, or small, quiet toys are good choices.

• Use your star charts and issue reminders before you go out to the restaurant. Be specific about what behavior is expected.

Shopping and errands

Errands, especially on weekends, seem to be the foundations of our lives. We have to run out to the store for milk, to drop one of our children at soccer practice, to buy a gift for a friend, to go to the dentist. And often there's no choice but to take a demanding child along—creating endless opportunities for stress and misbehavior.

Shopping for clothes can be a trying experience for the demanding child and for her parents. The high-energy child would rather do *anything* than try on shirts. The impulsive child wants everything she sees, and she wants it *now*. The angry child hates every dress you show her, and throws a tantrum in the store. And the persistent child knows exactly what she wants. She will accept no substitutes. She won't buy anything until you find that perfect jacket in the perfect shade of jade that doesn't seem to exist at the mall.

There are no easy answers for shopping nightmares with demanding children. As we said above, it may be helpful to depersonalize clothing issues as much as possible so that inappropriate choices don't upset you so much. It may help, also, to shop for clothing by yourself, buy several items, and have your child try them on and make her choices at home. Or have your child circle items in a catalog that she likes.

• Try to minimize the number of errands and the amount of time you spend on them. An entire Saturday spent racing around town jumping in and out of the car can be stressful for anyone, but especially a persistent child who has trouble with transitions.

• Auto safety is a non-negotiable issue. Make sure everyone obeys the rules about seat belts. High-energy kids may squirm and wiggle, but safety issues should not be a choice: they belong in the category of Essentials (Chapter 6).

• If the question of who gets to sit in the front seat is a contentious issue in your family, establish a schedule. You might rotate turns, make a chart, or—if you have just two children—alternate odd and even days.

• Stores are a prime setting for tantrums and whining. Prepare for shopping trips by repeating the rules and expectations for store behavior.

• If your young child tends to pull away from you, or grab items in a store or checkout line, get her in the habit of holding or touching something "magical" while you conduct your business. One mother of three young children is able to withdraw cash from an automatic teller machine without being distracted by asking her children to touch a letter on a nearby sign. "Keep your fingers on the 'E,' " she says. Another mother keeps a plastic toy that's just for stores. "Hang on to your turtle!" she reminds her wiggly son during shopping trips.

• Do not give in to checkout-line begging. If your child has a tantrum, leave the store and issue an age-appropriate consequence.

Vacations and trips

Often the parents of demanding children observe that their children seem to be at their best on vacations.

"Alan is at his best when we're traveling," said one mother. "I find vacations exhausting, but he loves our trips, and they bring out the best in him. The change of scene keeps him stimulated in a good way. He's never bored."

Vacations are exciting because they offer the change of scene that so many of us find refreshing and exciting. But for some demanding children, especially those who have difficulty with transitions, those changes create opportunities for conflict and complaint.

Vacations also offer endless trouble spots: long airplane rides to trap high-energy kids; dangers and breakables to tempt impulsive kids; stress, fatigue, and close quarters to set off angry kids.

And it's all even harder because fun times are *supposed* to be fun. You've invested time and money in the endeavor, and everyone has expectations for a good time.

Some suggestions for vacations:

• If bedtime tends to be a difficult time for your child, try to re-create familiar nighttime routines during the vacation. Pack your child's "blankie," a familiar pillow or pillow case, favorite bedtime books. Try to stay close to her usual bedtime.

• Fatigue is the enemy of self-control. Demanding children—even high-energy ones—do get tired. Remember that you don't have to do it all. Dragging a child through the Smithsonian, the Lincoln Memorial, the Capitol, and the National Gallery in one day may be a recipe for misery, not happy memories.

• Plan ahead for car and airplane trips, especially if your child has trouble sitting still. Bring a survival kit with books, quiet toys, and craft items.

• When visiting relatives, try for open communication about your child's temperament and behavior, just as you did with her teachers and coaches.

• Be prepared to be especially vigilant with your high-energy or impulsive child during outings and vacations. Changes of scene provide ripe opportunities for accidents and injuries, or just slipping away in a strange city and getting lost.

SPECIAL SITUATIONS

Demanding children who are learning to manage their own behavior quite well can become disorganized when a major life event takes place. When the family moves to a new city, or the child changes schools, or there's a divorce or a death, they can lose the equilibrium they've forged.

Moving

Moving to a new home can be difficult for demanding children. Changing homes is stressful for everyone, and demanding children have more difficulty behaving well when they are under extra stress.

And the break in routine can disrupt the routines that they have been using to gain control of their behavior. Most children are at their best when their lives are predictable. They're comforted by the routines and schedules of family life. So if the family moves to a new house or Mom gets a new job with different hours, the demanding child may become more demanding.

Do try to keep whatever routines you can, including bedtime and homework expectations, during the move. But don't expect perfection during a stressful time.

Demanding children often thrive on the kind of challenge that would upset more sensitive souls.

Moving to a new house or community can be an exciting adventure for a demanding child. She is likely to have plenty of energy for packing or moving and for rearranging her new room. She may be more outgoing and enthusiastic about her new home, and be more able to reach out and forge new friendships.

Guests

When Grandpa moves in to the home, or house guests come for a week, or step-siblings come to stay for the summer, it's particularly difficult for demanding children to keep their cool.

The angry child becomes angrier, the energetic child becomes wilder, and the persistent child becomes insatiable and needy.

Make an effort to ensure some privacy for your demanding child. If she has to share her room for a period of time, make a schedule so that during certain periods of time, she can be by herself, and during others, the guest can have private time.

A new baby

Like all children, your demanding child will require extra attention when a new baby enters the family. Her behavior may not be at its best during this transitional stage. Whatever her age, she'll need more patience, support, and affection from you.

Do allow your demanding child to express her views about the new arrival. Don't expect her to be entirely positive about having to share your affections with an infant. Be realistic about both the joys and troubles that new babies bring to a family.

When possible, channel her temperament traits into positive things she can do for the baby. Her energy will help you care for the baby by fetching diapers or toys, or, if she is older, pushing the stroller. Her persistence will keep her more interested in playing with the baby without getting bored.

Divorce

When parents divorce, children often find themselves spending part of their time with a noncustodial parent, or sharing their own home with half-siblings who visit. The change and readjustment involved can be difficult whether it's a weekend visit or an entire summer.

When parents share custody, it's more difficult to maintain the united front that is so helpful in managing demanding behavior. And issues of anger can arise, both in the hurt child and in the struggling custodial parent. Studies have shown that children of divorce do better when parents who are angry and hurt over the divorce are able to control their anger and limit their venting of grievances against the former spouses.

Whether the setting is school, an airplane flight, or a trip to the shopping mall, these areas of particular challenge are actually a whole series of "teachable moments" for demanding children. Every time your child masters a skill or conquers a difficult setting, she's learning to handle her temperament, to grow toward the capable adult she's destined to become. And that's what we'll discuss in the following chapter.

◆ 9 ◆

Looking Ahead:
What the Future Holds for Your
Demanding Child

One of the joys of parenthood is to imagine our child as an adult, fully grown, capable, successful, happy, and fulfilled.

We want that for them, because we love them. But we also look forward to the satisfaction that we've successfully fulfilled our responsibilities as parents.

But demanding children sometimes put our optimism to the test. It's hard to see beyond the daily struggles of parenthood and glimpse the possibilities. Yet it's essential to focus on the positive aspects of our demanding child's qualities. That way, we'll be more optimistic and less tense, and thus more able to be effective parents. And a positive attitude leaves us open to the delights and surprises that our children will bring us as they grow.

WHAT PARENTS WORRY ABOUT

All parents wonder about what the future holds for their children, whether those children are demanding or not. Will they manage to get through college—or even get *into* college? Will they have friends, fall in love, earn a living, succeed, be happy?

But the parents of demanding children have more specific worries. Theirs are the toddlers who bite and get banished from playgroup. Theirs grab and fidget in class, get into scuffles on the playground, and get called to the principal's office. Theirs are the children who throw tantrums in the supermarket, slam doors during arguments, and irritate their friends with their inflexibility.

How can my impulsive child who can't be trusted to take the china out of the dishwasher ever grow up to be a safe driver or operate power tools?

How will my child who seethes with anger learn to control his rages and stay out of trouble?

How will my child, who screams every time he loses at Sorry, ever learn to be a good sport?

How will my child's impulsiveness play out when he's a teenager?

My child gets so angry when things don't go her way. How will she form and maintain friendships? How will she work through the ups and downs of establishing a relationship?

How will my child learn to follow orders and take criticism in the workplace?

Sometimes, parental anxiety is greater when the parent and child share the same kind of demanding traits and the parent recalls suffering because of it. "He's so much like me. I remember how much trouble I got into when I was young. I don't want to even *think* about it!"

As we discussed in Chapter 3, parents worry that their child will suffer the same way they did, or miss out on opportunities in life the same way they did.

Parents also worry when they are strikingly different from their demanding children.

"I'm definitely not a risk-taker," says one father. "I'd worry about my son's well-being even if he were careful like me. But he's not. He's a daredevil. I don't know how I'll survive if he takes up sky-diving."

Parents who are consumed with anxiety about their children's futures are less able to concentrate on the ways they can help in the here and now. And too much parental fretting has another effect: It can can convey anxiety to the children, suggesting that parents have little faith in the children's ability to grow and thrive and overcome their difficulties.

The parents who keep their worries in perspective, then, are in the best position to parent positively. Usually, they are the ones who are either similar in temperament to their children, or who have come to understand, work with, and even celebrate their demanding child's individuality, even when child and parent are quite different.

Sometimes, the worries we have about our challenging children can be eased as they demonstrate their strengths. As they grow, they grow stronger—not always in ways that we are familiar with, but in their own unique way. Consider David's mother's story:

"With my older son, who is more sensitive, I had to put considerable effort into every outing or event to make him comfortable. I had to tend to his fears and his worries. But with Steven, I'm getting a free ride. He's so full of drive and pep, he's always ready for anything.

"For a long time, I was dwelling on how hard it was to keep him out of trouble, because he tends to plunge into new situations before he knows what he's doing. But as he's gotten older, I've started to see what a wonderful advantage those same traits are for him. He's ready for anything. We say, 'Well, Steve, do you want to go to soccer camp this summer? It's for a whole week. . . . ' And he says, 'Sure!' It will be the same when he goes off to college, or starts a job."

HOW DEMANDING CHILDREN GROW AND CHANGE

Demanding children have qualities common to children of all temperaments, except that they have them in excess. Physical energy, impulsiveness, difficulty inhibiting intense emotions, and stubborn or selfish behavior are traits that almost *define* childhood, and they modify as children become more mature. Demanding children have these traits in excess, but they will modify as well.

Jerome Kagan, the authority on temperament, has conducted extensive studies of temperament and its persistence in children. He and his colleagues report that among extremely shy eighteen-month-olds, about half are still extremely shy at age eight, and the rest fall into the average range. That would suggest that the behavior of these highly inhibited children can be modified by experience.

That contrasts with a group of uninhibited and outgoing toddlers. Of that group, 75 percent exhibit the same traits at age eight. A bold, extroverted temperament is more likely to persist than an inhibited, fearful temperament.

One reason for that persistence, Kagan suggests, is that many traits of bold, uninhibited children are positive qualities that bring encouragement and rewards as the child grows older. There's no *need* to stop being athletic and courageous, for example.

Let's look ahead to what the four categories of demanding behavior might look like as your child grows.

THE HIGH-ENERGY CHILD

• Your high-energy child won't always slam doors or be disruptive in the classroom, but chances are he'll always go through life with zest. The force will always be with him. He will slow down a bit, but he'll still seek out opportunities for physical activity. He may always be a toe-tapping, finger-drumming, keyed-up person. He'll be the adult who has to stand up when talking on the telephone.

THE IMPULSIVE CHILD

This trait does tend to modify with maturity. As he grows older, his impulsivity may turn into curiousity and a keen interest in new experiences and challenges. He won't be satisfied with things as they are, or with routines that he considers dull.

Instead of tossing the chocolate milk into his ears, your child may grow up to be an adult who seeks novelty and is willing to take calculated risks. He may be a contestant on *Jeopardy* who pushes the buzzer first. Your adult child may be uncomfortable with sameness: He'll paint the house a different color every two years and insist on going someplace new every year for vacation. He'll thrive on being spontaneous.

THE ANGRY CHILD

Traits like aggression and impulsivity if they continue into later life, without modification, put people at higher risk for dangerous or criminal behavior. But most children learn to control their aggressive tendencies. Your intense son probably won't be throwing tantrums in the candy aisle of the supermarket when he's forty, but he'll still respond to life's challenges with intensity. His reactions will always tend to be passionate, rather than measured and serene, and he'll always have to work harder to keep his emotional energy within acceptable bounds. But his anger, properly channeled, can become a passion for justice and an intense interest in righting wrongs.

THE PERSISTENT CHILD

Your persistent child probably will not grow up to be flexible and easygoing, but he may well transmute that stubborn quality into determination. He may be dogged in pursuit of his goals, and hard to deflect from his purpose. He'll stick with relationships, and work things through instead of giving up and leaving. He'll do the same with tasks and professional responsibilities, as well.

For this child, success in the future may lie in finding the right "rut." Once he finds a field where depth and persistence and a refusal to give up pay-off, he'll achieve great things.

Demanding children grow up into adults with strong, forceful personalities. Even under the worst of conditions, some of their rough edges would be smoothed off by experience and maturity, not to mention the complaints and criticisms of friends and sweethearts and employers. But under the best of conditions, demanding children modify their more troublesome traits and allow the finest ones to flourish.

Although temperament persists throughout life, its influence recedes somewhat in adulthood because it must compete with environment and experiences. The newborn baby is largely a biological creature. But a 25-year-old man is, whatever his innate temperament, to a great degree a product of his history.

By adulthood, we have either learned techniques for managing our temperament biases, or we have not. But ideally, we accommodate ourselves to our temperament just as water accommodates itself to the vessel in which it is held.

Temperament does endure. But how it persists, and in what form, is what you can influence. That's what this book has been all about.

THE DEMANDING ADOLESCENT

Adolescence is a challenging stage of life for any child, and that child's parents. But the parents of demanding children worry more than most. How, they wonder, will my child get along in school, stay out of trouble, and stay safe? And how will I be able to get along with my stubborn, intense child when he's bigger than me? How will I control my demanding child? How will we handle issues of power, freedom, responsibility, and conflict?

First, the negatives:
• An impulsive or high-energy adolescent may take more risks than other teenagers and need closer supervision. Mature privileges, like driving, need to be linked to demonstrated maturity, rather than age alone. Thus, an impulsive teenager might need more time than others to develop the respon-

sibility needed to drive a car safely or spend an unsupervised weekend.

• An angry, aggressive adolescent is at greater risk for violent or criminal behavior.

• A persistent teen may dig in his heels and be even more resistant to advice and guidance than most teenagers. He may remain in an unsatisfactory relationship from stubbornness rather than true love.

And now for the bright side:

In the first book in this series, *The Sensitive Child*, we addressed the worries that parents of children who are shy, anxious, and cautious have about their children's adolescence. Those parents worry about how their children will approach the opposite sex, stand up to the rigors of adolescence, speak up for themselves, and handle the stress and competition of the workplace.

As the parent of a demanding child, you can rejoice in the likelihood that you won't have to deal with those concerns.

• Demanding teenagers have the energy and daring to forge relationships, and the ability to recover from the inevitable romantic disappointments of youth.

• They have the energy, drive, and spirit to try out for the team or the school play, enter competitions, invite their friends to do things, ask someone out for a date.

• They stand up for their rights and complain with vigor when things aren't right.

• They don't suffer in silence. Chances are you'll

know when your demanding child is unhappy.

• Their passion and intensity helps parents know what's going on in their child's life.

As we discussed earlier, your child will gradually assume more of the tasks of managing his own temperament and behavior as he matures. More and more, you will step back and let your child take on responsibility for his own decisions and their consequences. And during your child's adolescence, your role changes, too: When he needs advice and support, he will turn as much to his peers as he does to you.

WHEN TO WORRY ABOUT YOUR DEMANDING CHILD

Negative self-image

Your child should—ideally—like himself enough as he is. But demanding traits can bruise a child's self-esteem, especially if they cause him to struggle in school or fail to establish friendships. If your child dwells relentlessly on his inadequacies, if he is constantly putting himself down, he may need evaluation and support from a therapist.

Once he reaches adolescence, your demanding child may join the ranks of typical teenagers who go through a breast-beating stage that isn't necessarily out of the ordinary. For normal teens (whether demanding or not), those stages limit themselves, and are balanced with periods of confidence and good cheer.

Extreme reactions

Are your child's emotional reactions out of all proportion? Does he rage and storm all day long? Is his aggression frightening to you and to him? By now, you know what level of intensity is typical of your child, and you will be able to see if it's getting more so.

With normal children—even demanding ones—even a powerful negative reaction eventually fades. If your child responds to difficulties in ways that seem seriously out of proportion, he may feel overwhelmed by his troubles and benefit from outside help.

Secondary effects

Sometimes a demanding child's troubles reach beyond temperament and generate effects in far-reaching areas of life—and affect others beyond himself.

Is your child's health and safety being affected? Is he getting hurt too often?

Are his behavioral problems in school affecting his school attendance, his ability to learn, his opportunities for growth?

Is your child's behavior cutting him off from experiences he needs?

Are your demanding child's troubles having a negative effect on other familiy members? Are your other children developing problems and anxieties because of the tensions in the family? If a child needs so much attention and help that another child is neglected, for example, the family may need outside help and support.

Thoughts of suicide

Is your demanding child discussing suicide? Many children who are not deeply troubled do sometimes say, "I'll kill myself" when frustrated or angry. Even if they seem trivial, those comments should be listened to and responded to in a caring way. But an unhappy child who discusses suicide should be evaluated professionally.

If you feel that your demanding child is struggling desperately, or if you yourself are struggling with anxiety, anger, or fatigue, do seek support. You might start with your pediatrician, who can recommend a therapist who works with families and children. Try to find a therapist who understands and honors temperament, and is willing to work within the context of your child's unique traits.

DEMANDING ADULTS

"The longest weekend of my life was during this winter's blizzard. I was stuck at home, and after I'd cleaned the house and rearranged all the closets, I thought I'd go crazy. I went in to work before the streets were plowed. My boss was very impressed. But I *have* to be busy."

"Once I've made a decision, I have to act. It's very difficult for me to wait for anything. My wife and I are looking for a house, and every time we see something we like, I'm ready to make an offer right away. I'm ready to get moving. But my wife insists on thinking it over. She's probably right, but I find it frustrating."

"I know I have a short temper, but at least my friends always know where I stand."

"Once I've started a job, I can't give up until it's finished. I'm the only father in my neighborhood who always finishes every home-improvement project I start. It's not that I'm virtuous; it's just that I can't stop thinking about it until it's done."

We can usually tell where demanding adults stand. They refuse to fade into the woodwork. They stand out from their more easygoing peers because they're particularly hardworking, ambitious, courageous, and clear about their goals.

They are the high-energy people who are incredibly productive for the simple reason that they get more done than their more languid brethren. This trait fuels the entrepreneurial drive that launches new businesses. Inexhaustible energy underlies careers in sports, finance, and politics.

The daring child becomes the courageous adult who puts out forest fires, tests airplanes, or blasts off in the space shuttle. Your impulsive child may not grow up to travel in space, but he'll probably be the kind of adult who is capable of acting decisively.

The intense, easily angered child becomes the prophet or reformer whose passion motivates and inspires others.

As adults, persistent children are single-minded and don't wilt in the face of opposition. That same determination that made bedtime so infuriating when your child was three may make his competitors and adversaries crumble when he is thirty.

The persistent child who has trouble with change may become a focused, committed scholar, scientist, or community leader.

When he combines that determination with energy and emotional intensity, he may become a political leader who needs that "fire in the belly" in order to face the challenges of campaigning and governing.

Demanding children, as adults, are the people who change history and figure as memorable figures in literature because of the power of their personalities. In this group, you'd be likely to find Julius Caesar but not Hamlet.

You'd find Sir Walter Raleigh but not John Milton.

You'd be more likely to find Katherine Hepburn than Audrey Hepburn, John McEnroe than Boris Becker.

You'd find someone like Winston Churchill, who was a disruptive, hyperactive child but grew up to lead his nation heroically. You'd find someone like Pablo Picasso, who from childhood was intense and stubborn in the pursuit of his art. Ingmar Bergman and Bob Dylan were defiant, disobedient children. Yet all survived, thrived, and changed the world.

As adults, demanding people might be described as:

- Creative
- Ambitious
- Hard-working and energetic
- Courageous and valiant
- Focused and dedicated
- Adventurous
- Determined
- Independent
- Principled

These traits come with a price, as any parent of a demanding child can attest. But they are honorable qualities that have a special place in human history.

As one teacher who has seen hundreds of children pass through her doors puts it, "We need all kinds of people. We need shy people, we need loud people, we need boisterous people. If they're shy, I want to modify their shyness. If they're impulsive, I want to help them get control. But I don't try to change their personality. My job is to respect who they are."

Your demanding child has qualities that the world needs. He has the drive, the ambition, the determination, the zest, and the sheer energy to take on challenges, to pour his energy into a solution, and, ultimately, to prevail. As you know from intimate experience, he is not easily thwarted, and he's hard to stop.

These qualities are his legacy, and your challenge is to bring up your child in such a way that he doesn't lose this gift but emerges from childhood still in possession of his unique birthright.

◇ **10** ◇

Questions and Answers

Q: *Why does my demanding child behave so much better for his father than he does for me? I feel as though I'm using all my power to get him to budge, and the most ordinary little conflicts escalate into exhausting battles. But his father asks him to do something and he does it willingly and respectfully!*

A: There may be a better fit between your son and your husband than between your son and you, either because their temperaments are similar or because they have established an easy rapport. There may not be much you can do about the chemistry that underlies this three-way relationship.

Sometimes, also, children respond more readily to a father who angers easily. If your husband uses anger, or the threat of anger, to get your son to behave, and you try to compensate by being lenient, you're sending a mixed message.

As to what *can* be done, it's important to enlist your husband's support. It's natural for the more successful parent to take pride in his skills. Sometimes, however, that leads to a subtle undermining of the other parent's efforts at managing the child's behavior. Or you may be resentful of your husband's success and do some undermining of your own.

Whatever the specifics, it's important that the two of you work together. Go over your priorities and house rules first with your husband, to make sure you're in agreement. Then present a united front to your son. Your husband should insist that your son treat you respectfully, and that he follow the family expectations for courtesy.

The fact that your son is able to behave well for your husband is, of course, evidence that he's capable of controlling his conduct when he's motivated.

Q: *I love my children, but I find it hard sometimes to be as loving toward my son, who is very outgoing and energetic, as toward my daughter. I know his qualities are going to help him over time, but I have trouble being positive about him because I am shy and introverted. My daughter is more like me, and we get along so effortlessly. I run out of patience more easily with my son than my daughter, even when he hasn't done anything wrong. How can I develop an accepting attitude toward both my children?*

A: Accept that is possible to love your children differently. This means that in some situations, or at certain times, you may feel more love for one child and less for the other.

You may, for example, have great rapport with

one child while you're working companionably in the kitchen, but your heart will fill with love for your demanding child as you watch him stride to the front of the school auditorium, take the steps two at a time, and belt out a comedy song for the talent show.

Loving our children fairly does not mean loving them in exactly the same way, any more than treating them fairly means treating them identically.

Q: *My eight-year-old son is incredibly stubborn. He resists everything I tell him to do without even thinking about it. It's like a reflex. I know I need to give him limits and structure, but everything I try generates his stubbornness. He either resists entirely, or says he's finished with a chore or his homework when he isn't. Eventually, I get so exhausted that I figure, "Is this worth it?" and back off some of my demands. What else can I try?*

A: Often we and our demanding children can both get overwhelmed by the sheer number of behaviors that need improvement. When we try to do everything at once, the task seems insurmountable. Could it be that you are working on too many areas at once, and your son is tuning you out for that reason? We've discussed the importance of setting priorities in Chapter 6.

If you believe you've narrowed your rules down to the essentials, and your son still is not showing any ownership of the problem, try transferring your control system from your own voice to a less personal medium. If you write down the things he needs to do on a list, and have him check them off when he's finished, you'll find yourself nagging less. Reward charts help, too, because your son will be working toward an objective goal, rather than doing something in order to please you or get you to stop being angry. By taking some of the emotional content out of the rules, you can reduce the "reflex" behavior.

Even at eight, your son may be ready to participate more in the management of his own behavior. As he grows older, he'll be better able to use his own strengths and stubborn determination constructively.

Q: *My impulsive daughter won't stick with any effort long enough to get the results and rewards that would encourage her. She's starting piano lessons this year, and she's ready to quit after a few weeks because she says she "stinks" at it. She hardly practices at all because she says, "It's too hard" or "I stink at piano." How can I teach her persistence?*

A: Reward her when she shows small steps in the right direction. Her own actions won't result in great rewards for a long time, so you need to provide the rewards. You might try a chart system, as discussed in Chapter 6.

This is another example of a situation in which natural consequences may not be adequate to the task. Your daughter won't stick to anything long enough to get those rewards, so you have to intervene with more artificial reinforcements for the time being.

Piano may be a particularly challenging choice for a child like yours, because it requires consid-

erable effort and dedication before results are forth-
coming. You might try using your reward chart to
track her practices, such as the length of time she
practices or the number of times she practices a
particular piece. If she practices diligently for a
week, she might earn an outing or a treat. In that
way, her efforts will result in rewards, even before
her piano playing becomes proficient and satisfying enough to provide its own reward.

Q: *How can I talk to my nine-year-old son about his
anger? I know that when he's furious and upset is not
the time to try to get him to explain what's behind his
anger. But even when we're both calm, if I bring up the
subject of his temperament, and try to get him to talk
about his feelings, he gets angry and won't talk about
it. I find myself so grateful for those moments when he's
not angry that I am reluctant to spoil the mood by talking about difficult topics.*

A: If you think your son's angry feelings need
to be examined and evaluated, it might be helpful
to have someone else take that role. It may be too
difficult for your son to reveal his troubling emotions to you. Another family member or a therapist
might take on this role more effectively.

Your communication with your son may improve if you retreat a bit. You may be pushing him
to reveal his feelings. When your son does talk
about any feelings—angry or otherwise—listen
with your full attention, but restrain your desire to
assess or judge his emotions. Resist the desire to
fire questions at him, issue instant advice, or give
him an uplifting lesson every time he talks.

If your son says something like, "That new kid is a jerk," you might be tempted to say, "That's not a very nice thing to say," or "I'm sure if you give him a chance, he'll be okay."

Instead, you can reflect back what he says: "Sounds like he does things that bug you." A simple statement like that indicates that his emotional message has been received, and paves the way for further communication.

Q: *When I was growing up, we were "yellers." We all showed our feelings in my family. When we got mad, we said what was on our mind, and when we were having fun, we showed that, too. We all turned out fine. Isn't it better to scream and clear the air than to hold in honest feelings?*

A: The kind of family dynamic you describe can be healthy and successful if it's working for every family member. There are traditions and cultures in which it's natural to communicate with more energy and noise, and the volume level doesn't have much to do with hostility. The problem can occur when one family member is not comfortable with this style. Also, even when it's working well within the family, children need to learn techniques of getting along in the greater culture. Children who are noisy and explosive in the family setting may not be able to tone down their approach in other settings where their habits may be a disadvantage.

Q: *My son has a mean streak when he's really angry. He lashes out and says "I hate you!" as though he really wants to hurt my feelings. The other day he said I was* *fat, and I know he did it just to be mean. How can I "emphasize behavior and not the motive" when his motive seems so hurtful?*

A: Even though your son seems to be trying to hurt your feelings, it will be more profitable for you to focus on what he has done than on his intentions. If he says things designed to be hurtful, then he is being verbally abusive. You need to invoke your rules against verbal attack. If he says, "You meanie!" during an argument, you can go over to the behavior chart and say, "Let's see. Name Calling: It says here the penalty is scrubbing the trash cans."

If his behavior doesn't call for a specific penalty, you can still say, "I don't like hearing that. I don't think that you and I are ready to discuss this reasonably. We can talk again later."

The chances are that your son's fundamental motive for his provoking behavior is not to be awful, but to get a vigorous response from you. He has probably learned that you hate being called mean, or fat, and that doing so guarantees a lively response from you. The more you respond calmly and consistently, the more you will reduce the payoff for him.

Q: *How can I tell if my son's endless energy is really unusual, or if it's par for the course for three-year-olds? What are the signs?*

A: Trying to identify a toddler or preschooler as "high energy" is certainly difficult, since most children this age fill the bill much of the time. The important distinction to look for is how your son compares to other children his age, and in the same setting.

You can do this by observing him in group settings where he's with his age-mates, such as at his day-care center, at a playground, or at the beach. When you take him to the play area at the park, for example, is he the loudest child there? Does his day-care teacher identify him as one of the most physically active children in the group?

Think back, also, to his infancy—and even before. Did he kick a lot before birth? Was he always wiggly and unwilling to sit still? Did he seem to need less sleep? High energy as a temperamental trait is likely to be present throughout life, rather than show up out of the blue in the toddler years.

Q: *My five-year-old constantly interrupts. When I'm on the phone, or trying to hold a conversation with an adult, she won't leave me alone. She says "Mommy!" all the time, even if she doesn't really need anything or have an important question. She'll make noise right near the phone just to distract me. If I try ignoring her when she does this, she keeps it up until I can't continue my conversation.*

A: If you get into a contest with a persistent child to see who can outwait whom, chances are you'll lose. If you rely on ignoring intrusive or interrupting behavior, it won't improve. And if you just yell, or reprimand your daughter without following through, her behavior will earn her your attention, which is what she's seeking.

You may need to put "interrupting" high on your priorities list, and concentrate on helping your child improve her behavior on this issue. Tell her clearly what the rules are, and why interrupting is not allowed except in true emergencies. Next time you make a phone call, set a timer and explain to her that she needs to amuse herself quietly until the timer rings. If she is able to do that, then you'll play a game together. Keep your conversations short for a while, to make it easier for your daughter to succeed.

If she continues to interrupt you, issue an appropriate consequence. Respond immediately to the interruption, but do not respond to what she asks for. If she tugs at your sleeve and says, "Mommy, what's for dinner? What's for dinner?" do not say, "Tacos! Now, will you leave me alone?" Instead, say, "You're interrupting. We'll talk about the consequence for interrupting when I'm finished on the phone."

Q: *How can I establish consistent discipline with my two children who have dramatically different temperaments? My ten-year-old son is quiet and gets upset and anxious easily. He needs very little punishment, since he's usually well-behaved. My daughter, who's seven, is just the opposite. She's impulsive and aggressive and gets into more trouble than my son. Then when I reprimand her or take away privileges, she says I'm tougher on her than on her brother.*

A: The chances are that your daughter would find an opportunity to accuse you of unfairness even if their temperament, behavior and treatment were absolutely identical. That's the nature of siblings.

Your best bet is to convey to your children that they are individuals and respond to limits and punishments differently. You can discuss temperament with your children, so that they understand their own strengths and limitations, and well as the strengths and limitations of the other.

However, in matters of discipline, it's more important to look beyond temperament and concentrate on behavior. If your demanding child really does misbehave more, then you are on solid ground in explaining that she brings more punishment upon herself for that reason.

Take care, however, that your explanation doesn't come out as a comparison with her "better" brother. You don't want to say, "If you were more like Zach, you wouldn't be in trouble all the time." Point out to her that if she chooses to behave badly, she brings on her own negative consequences.

Q: *My husband is very impatient with our daughter. If she pesters him at all, he gets fed up immediately. He's not interested in understanding her temperament. He says I'm too lenient and let her get away with too much. I know our daughter is no angel. She knows what she wants, and she will make a scene until she gets it. But I think she needs to be loved and accepted for what she is, rather than made to conform to what society expects of her.*

A: It's difficult to direct a demanding child's development when parents take dissimilar views. You both are partly right, in that your child needs both acceptance *and* limits. Together, try to forge a compromise that includes both these elements.

Your husband may feel more willing to praise your daughter if he feels you will support him on conduct issues. And you may feel more comfortable sticking to your guns on discipline issues if you feel your husband is meeting your daughter's needs for her father's love and acceptance. Once you're in agreement, present a united front to your daughter.

Consider, also, that if your husband finds your daughter's behavior annoying, the likelihood is that other people will, too. That's a good reason to look for ways to modify her habits. You aren't doing your daughter a favor by allowing her to continue behaviors that will make her less welcome in the world at large.

Q: *I understand that temperament may have a genetic component. Does this mean that certain temperaments run in families? It seems that most families I know have children with quite different personalities.*

A: People in families are not identical. No two have the same set of genes, unless they are identical twins. The number of possible combinations of traits that two parents could generate is limited only by the number of children they have. Even closely related people have different hair color, eye color, nose shape, height, just as they have different interests, talents, and temperaments.

Q: *I'm not sure I'm comfortable with identifying my son as "angry" or "demanding" when I'm explaining him to other people, other parents in particular. If he's just misbehaved, and I start explaining his temperament,* *it sounds as if I'm excusing him. How can I explain him better?*

A: It's true that just announcing a label to describe your child can come off as overly indulgent, especially if your child is repeating his misbehavior and you tell others that he is "determined."

It's probably more helpful to use terms that describe what your child does, and how he's likely to react. If your persistent son is about to spend the day at a friend's house, you might tell the parent, "Mark sometimes has trouble changing gears when he's set on doing something. If the children are playing outside, it may be hard to get him to come in for lunch. We've found that if Mark doesn't come in when we call him, he'll respond if we begin a countdown: We start at ten, then count backward toward "blast-off." He usually cooperates just before we get to 'zero.'"

When you discuss your demanding child with other parents in that way, it does two things: First, it educates them about Mark's personality, and gives them a practical tip on how to work with him. Second, it reassures them that you're aware of the parts of his temperament that need management, and that you're working on them.

Q: *My son is adopted. His temperament is very different from mine. Will we have a harder time establishing a good fit?*

A: There will be many traits that differ between you and your son, including appearance and medical history. And certainly the aspects of his temperament that are genetic won't match yours.

However, many children differ greatly in temperament from their biological parents, as you can observe all around you. And children also differ considerably from their biological siblings as well. In all families, parents delight in traits that surprise them, qualities they never expected to see in their children.

You should be able to understand and celebrate your son's individuality and his temperament by using the same suggestions and techniques that apply to all families.

Q: *My daughter's tantrums seem different now that she's four. Before, when she got mad and started screaming and throwing things, she seemed truly unhappy. I would try to comfort her and get her to relax. But now, the more I try to calm her down, the worse she gets. She doesn't settle down until I give in to what she wants.*

A: It's important to distinguish between emotional tantrums and manipulative tantrums. Angry children, when they are toddlers, may have frequent episodes of rage and loss of control that emerge largely from their inability to manage intense emotions. These tantrums usually occur in response to frustration, or when the child is particularly tired.

Later, as children get more mature, there is a greater element of learning and calculation in tantrums. If children are energetic, angry, or persistent, you can see how those temperament traits can play out in a tantrum.

Remember that angry children continue to be angry because they have found that it gets results.

The more reward there is for the angry behavior, the less motivation there is for learning alternate ways of communicating feelings and frustrations.

Earlier, you handled your daughter's emotional tantrums in a way that was appropriate for her age. Now that she's older, your approach needs to evolve with her. Now, you need to focus on tantrums as a behavior issue as well as an emotional one.

You can remind your daughter that she's old enough now to explain what she needs with words. You can tell her that if she screams and fusses, she'll have to go somewhere by herself until she can cool down (or you can issue a time-out). And, finally, you can make sure that she does not get rewarded for her loss of control, whether it's at the toy store or at home with the family.

Q: *My five-year-old son is very physically active, and my husband and I are both comfortable with his energy. We spend plenty of time riding bikes, going to the playground and roughhousing at home. Our house is "child-friendly," and Jared has plenty of freedom to move during the day. But there are times when it's too much for me to keep up with him, and this is especially true on weekends. I have so much that I need to get done, and he wants me to stop what I'm doing and chase him around the yard. I get tired and impatient if I have to try to keep up with him, and then I get less tolerant of him and start resenting those same energetic qualities that I normally admire. What can I do?*

A: Try to arrange a little respite time for yourself. If you're spending positive time with your energetic son, and he still needs more action, someone else can take some of the pressure off you while you rest or get chores done.

Baby-sitters can provide welcome relief. But you might also consider hiring a neighborhood child who may not be old enough to baby-sit alone, but can still provide a few hours of responsible companionship for your son. While you remain at home to keep an eye on things, this ten- or eleven-year-old child can play ball with your son, play tag, or play board games or video games. Sometimes a young person is more willing to engage in the sort of energetic and silly play that five-year-olds enjoy so much. Usually a "mother's helper" gets paid less than a baby-sitter, since you are present and the child does not have full child-care responsibility.

Q: *My nine-year-old daughter is a great sulker. She picks the weekends when I have visitation with her to be impossible to please. If I ask her what she wants to do or where she wants to go, she can't think of anything. Then when I suggest something, she doesn't like my suggestions. This really gets my goat, because I know my daughter needs my presence in her life. I try to be available to my daughter on these occasions, and I hate to waste them.*

A: If your daughter's mood is always somewhat subdued and negative, that may just be her style. A child's usual mood is a temperament trait, and unlikely to change dramatically. But it's more likely that her behavior has a manipulative element. She may be resentful about her parents' separation, and be punishing you for your absence by refusing to cooperate when you are available.

If your daughter is coping reasonably well emotionally with the divorce and your focus is on improving her immediate behavior, you'll need to put the responsibility for having fun in her hands, not yours. Before your next visit, ask her to make a list of things she'd like to do. Then when you get together, you and she can select something from that list.

If she still refuses to be pleased, hide your annoyance and agree to spend time doing nothing. You may end up watching television or doing errands around town. It may not prove to be the quality time you'd hoped for. But when the pressure is off you to provide enjoyment, your daughter may be more willing to enjoy herself.

Q: *How much should I push my son to participate in activities that he isn't enthusiastic about? He tends to be angry and defiant, and my husband and I are trying to set priorities about when he absolutely has to do what we want, and when it's not so important. Recently, we wanted to go out to a restaurant for Sunday brunch. But our son said he didn't want to go—and we didn't. Was it a mistake to give in to him?*

A: Probably not. In this situation, setting priorities makes sense. The brunch outing was optional—one of those negotiable issues we discussed in Chapter 6. Disappointed as you may have been at not going out that morning, there was no harm in yielding to him on this occasion. Then, when there comes a time when he really *must* participate, like a family gathering or a holiday event, you are justified in requiring his cooperation.

Q: *My eight-year-old son and I were visiting friends recently when he and the little girl got into an argument. The kids were taunting each other, and finally my son threw a rock at her. At my insistence, he muttered a quick "Sorry." Then we went home. He lost his television privileges as a consequence.*

My son has a hot temper, but he isn't usually aggressive. What can I do to mend fences with his hosts?

A: One thing you might do is insist he write a letter of apology to the girl and the family. His letter could say that he's sorry he threw the rock, that he realizes that it hurt her, and that he's learned his lesson. He could mail the letter, although in-person delivery makes more of an impact on him and on the victims.

The letter-writing process serves several purposes:

First, it helps your son verbalize just what he did that was wrong, and underscores how serious the matter is.

Second, it brings a sense of closure: He has taken his punishment, he has issued an apology, and he can now move on.

And, third, a formal apology from a child can be quite effective. It's hard to stay angry at someone who apologizes, and it's even harder to stay mad at a child who shows up at your door with a letter telling how sorry he is.

Q: *Recently, my eight-year-old daughter had two friends over for the day. The girls started out playing* *pleasantly, but by lunchtime they were at each other's throats. My daughter is persistent and energetic, and wants to be the leader or the winner in every game. The other girls were refusing to go along with her, and every activity ended up with tears and squabbling. How can I avoid a repeat?*

A: Arranging social occasions for demanding children can take more planning and more supervision than might be the case with most children. Take into account these crucial elements, and choose them with care:

• The number and ages of the children. Usually, the fewer children the better. Even-numbered groups may get along better than odd numbers, because it's less likely that one child will feel excluded. If your child tries to dominate others, arrange a play experience with a somewhat older child, who will be less likely to be pushed around.

• The setting. An outdoor area, like a yard or a park playground, may be a better choice for active children than an apartment living room.

• The activities. If the children need lots of physical activity to remain on an even keel, set up a Ping-Pong table or arrange a treasure hunt or relay races. On the other hand, if your child and her friends become upset in competitive situations, consider cooperative games or craft activities.

Once you have everything arranged (with your child's input, of course), prepare her for the event. Remind her about the rules, and what behavior you expect from her and her friends.

And do expect to be available to supervise and direct to some degree. Just because other eight-year-olds play happily for hours with no adult involvement doesn't mean your demanding child is capable of that yet. Your involvement may be limited to checking on the children from time to time, but you should monitor their play so that if disputes develop, you can help them solve their problems with less hostility.

JANET POLAND is a writer, poet, and former newspaper editor who has written extensively about families and children for newspapers and magazines.

She graduated from Grinnell College and earned a graduate degree in political science from the University of Wisconsin. She worked in state government and in public television for several years before beginning a career in journalism. For more than a decade, she was a reporter, columnist, and editor on the staff of several daily newspapers in Pennsylvania, and received numerous journalism awards. More recently, as a free-lance journalist, her work has appeared frequently in the *Philadelphia Inquirer*.

She lives in Bucks County, Pennsylvania, with her husband and two sons.

JUDI CRAIG, PH.D., has counseled thousands of parents and children in more than twenty-seven years as a clinical psychologist. Readers are delighted with the common-sense approach of her most recent books, *Little Kids, Big Questions* and *Parents on the Spot*. Her "Parent Skills" column was featured for eight years in the *Sunday San Antonio Light*; her new column "Family Matters" appears in *Images*, a Sunday magazine in the *San Antonio Express News*. She has also consulted to corporations, agencies, schools, and psychiatric hospitals, and recently completed her training as a Master Practitioner in Neurolinguistic Programming. She is a frequent guest on national radio and television. She is the mother of three grown children, and lives in San Antonio, Texas.